Hell to Pay

Hell to Pay

HELLS ANGELS
VS.
THE MILLION-DOLLAR RAT

NEAL HALL

John Wiley & Sons Canada, Ltd.

Library and Archives Canada Cataloguing in Publication Data

Hall, Neal
    Hell to pay : Hells Angels vs. the million-dollar rat / Neal Hall.

Includes index.
ISBN 978-0-470-68096-4

    1. Hells Angels. 2. Plante, Michael. 3. Gang members—British Columbia—Vancouver. 4. Motorcycle gangs—British Columbia—Vancouver. 5. Informers—British Columbia—Vancouver.
6. Trials—British Columbia—Vancouver. 7. Organized crime investigation—British Columbia—Vancouver. I. Title.

HV6491.C32B75 2011   364.106'60971133   C2010-906945-5

ISBN 978-0-470-96401-9 (ePDF); 978-0-470-96399-9 (eMobi);
978-0-470-96400-2 (ePUB)

Production Credits
Cover design: Natalia Burobina
Interior text design: Mike Chan
Typesetter: Laserwords Pvt. Ltd.
Printer: Friesens

John Wiley & Sons Canada, Ltd.
6045 Freemont Blvd.
Mississauga, Ontario
L5R 4J3

Printed in Canada
1 2 3 4 5 FP 15 14 13 12 11

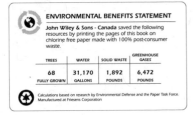

ENVIRONMENTAL BENEFITS STATEMENT

John Wiley & Sons - Canada saved the following resources by printing the pages of this book on chlorine free paper made with 100% post-consumer waste.

TREES	WATER	SOLID WASTE	GREENHOUSE GASES
68	31,170	1,892	6,472
FULLY GROWN	GALLONS	POUNDS	POUNDS

Calculations based on research by Environmental Defense and the Paper Task Force.
Manufactured at Friesens Corporation

To my family and my friends who grew up in Vancouver's East End.

CONTENTS

ACKNOWLEDGMENTS

I would like to thank the team at John Wiley & Sons Canada, among them editor Don Loney for first proposing this book and for his patience as the work progressed; project editor Elizabeth McCurdy for ushering it through to publication; and the deft editing of Jane Withey.

I also would like to thank my editors at the *Vancouver Sun* for allowing me the time away from work to write this book.

And thanks to my colleagues who covered this story with me over the years: Kim Bolan, Chad Skelton and Lori Culbert at the *Vancouver Sun*, and Keith Fraser at *The Province*.

Like most complex cases, it took five years for this prosecution to finally come to an end (with one key appeal still outstanding by February 2011). Any errors or omissions are my own.

LIST OF PRINCIPAL CHARACTERS

Rick **Alexander**—Hells Angels associate.

Robert **Alvarez**—Full-patch member of Hells Angels and member of the Nomads.

Wissam (Sam) Mohamed **Ayach**—Drug trafficker for Vancouver East End Hells Angels.

Benjamin **Azeroual**—Associate of the Vancouver East End chapter.

Chad James **Barroby**—Associate of the Vancouver East End chapter.

Jason William **Brown**—Associate of the Vancouver East End chapter.

John Peter **Bryce**—Chapter president, Vancouver East End chapter of the Hells Angels.

Jonathan Sal **Bryce Jr.**—Son of East End chapter president John Bryce.

Michael (Speedy) **Christiansen**—Hells Angels member and founding member of Halifax's 13th Tribe biker gang.

Claude **Duboc**—Drug lord whose underlings in B.C. collaborated with the Hells Angels.

Nima Abbassian **Ghavami**—A friend of Michael Plante and associate of the Vancouver East End chapter of the Hells Angels.

David Francis (Gyrator) **Giles**—Long-time Hells Angels member in Vancouver and formerly a member of the Hells Angels in Sherbrooke, Quebec.

Stanley Thomas **Gillis**—Sergeant at arms for the Vancouver East End chapter.

Richard **Goldammer**—Hells Angels member based in Kelowna, B.C.

Jamie **Holland**—Full-patch Hells Angel and member of the Nomads.

Brian **Jung**—Associate of the Vancouver East End chapter of the Hells Angels.

Norman Edward **Krogstad**—Former president of the Vancouver Hells Angels and the highest-ranking Hells Angels member to be convicted of drug trafficking in B.C.

Ronaldo **Lising**—Full-patch Hells Angel and member of the Nomads.

Villy Roy **Lynnerup**—Sergeant at arms of the Hells Angels White Rock, B.C. chapter.

David Patrick **O'Hara**—Former Vancouver and Mission, B.C. Hells Angels member.

David Ronald **Pearse**—An associate of the Vancouver East End chapter of the Hells Angels.

Leroy Serra **Pereira**—A childhood friend of John Punko and associate of the East End chapter.

Francisco Batista (Chico) **Pires**—Hells Angels member and a member of the Nomads.

George **Pires**—Full-patch member of the Hells Angels and member of the Nomads.

Michael **Plante**—Informant for the RCMP who was also an official friend of the Hells Angels. He was promised a total of $1 million to testify against former Hells Angels associates.

Randall (Randy) Richard **Potts**—Full-patch member of the Vancouver East End chapter of the Hells Angels.

John Virgil **Punko**—Hells Angels member of the Vancouver East End chapter.

Richard Andrew **Rempel**—Associate of the East End chapter.

Kerry Ryan **Renaud**—Associate of the East End chapter.

David Roger (Baldy) **Revell**—Hells Angels associate of the East End chapter.

Lloyd (Louie) George **Robinson**—Senior member of the Vancouver Hells Angels and half-brother of John Bryce.

Guy (Bully) **Rossignol**—Hells Angels member based in Kelowna, B.C.

Joseph Bruce **Skreptak**—Full-patch member of the Hells Angels based in Kelowna, B.C.

Cedric Baxter **Smith**—Senior Hells Angels member, missing and presumed dead since 2008.

Mickie (Phil) **Smith**—Contract killer convicted of five murders, including one for East End Hells Angels.

Juel (Jules) Ross **Stanton**—Hells Angels member, known for his violence. Nickname was Hooligan.

Tony **Terezakis**—Hells Angels associate.

Robert Leonard **Thomas,** aka Tattoo Rob—Hells Angels member.

Jean Joseph **Violette**—Full-patch member of the Vancouver Hells Angels.

Gino **Zumpano**—Full-patch member of the Hells Angels and member of the Nomads.

INTRODUCTION

In his youth, he was known as Big Mike, mainly because of his bulging biceps and chest muscles. He was also known as Sherman because he was built like a Sherman tank.

In 2002, the stocky weightlifter, Michael Dollard Plante, began working as a bouncer at Vancouver's Marble Arch strip club—a job he got with the help of an aspiring Hells Angels member named Randy Potts. At the time, Potts was in the Hells Angels "program"—the four-step process to attaining full membership in the world's most notorious outlaw motorcycle gang.

Plante often exchanged small talk with bikers at his local gym and, over time, began working out with members of Vancouver's East End chapter of the Hells Angels. Eventually he began advising them on weightlifting regimens to help them bulk up their bodies, as well as supplying them will illegal steroids.

One of them, Lloyd "Louie" George Robinson, invited Plante to lift weights with him at the East End chapter clubhouse, which was located on East Georgia Street. Robinson, then in his mid-40s, was a senior member of the East End Hells Angels and his half-brother, John Peter Bryce, was the chapter president.*

The Hells Angels, whose first chapter was established in Oakland, California, now has chapters spanning the globe. The Angels first began spreading their tentacles into Canada in the

---

* Robinson retired from the Hells Angels after charges were laid at the end of this investigation.

1970s, expanding across the country and eventually establishing more than 30 chapters. The East End chapter, considered one of the wealthiest and most powerful chapters in the country, was founded in 1983, when a local biker gang, the Satan's Angels, with three chapters in the Vancouver area and one in Nanaimo on Vancouver Island, were "patched over" to become part of the Hells Angels.

The bikers' lair was the East End clubhouse, fortified with surveillance cameras and steel doors with numeric keypads. It contained a private bar, lounge, meeting room, two bedrooms and a full gym.

Robinson, impressed by the results of his body-building buddy, began asking Plante to be his "spotter" during weightlifting sessions. At one point, Plante watched Robinson bench-press more than 400 pounds. His Hells Angels colleagues were impressed.

Plante soon gained a reputation as a reliable friend of the Hells Angels and they began throwing extra work his way. In addition to his job as a bouncer at the Marble Arch, after hours Plante worked as an "enforcer" for the bikers, acting as the hired muscle on debt collections to help intimidate people who owed money. His job was to convince debtors that they would have a lot less grief—and pain—if they simply paid up.

Often all it took was a mean look and even meaner threats, but, if necessary, he would use force to get people to pay what they owed. Sometimes he packed a gun. In January 2003, he went to threaten a man who had stolen Randy Potts' "hangaround vest." When the thief emerged from his house, Plante fired a .45-caliber pistol in the air three times. "I had gone there to scare him, bluff him out," Plante recalled, adding that he wore a balaclava so he could not be identified.

While Plante's career path involved seven assaults, most of the witnesses seemed to get cold feet and refused to report the matters to police. He did have one conviction for assaulting a man at a gym.

Then came the event that proved pivotal in his decision to become a police mole.

In July 2003, Plante, then 36, was asked to visit the office of James Betnar, a Vancouver businessman whom police believed owed $20,000 to David Patrick O'Hara. At the time, O'Hara was a Hells Angels member with the Mission chapter located outside of Vancouver.*

It started off as a routine assignment. Plante was asked by Randy Potts to pick up Betnar at his downtown office and take him to O'Hara's home in the Vancouver suburb of Surrey to enforce the collection. The 40-minute drive was tense and quiet. Betnar, knowing the fate that awaited him, said very little. Plante drove to O'Hara's expansive home and parked outside a large workshop where O'Hara worked on motorcycles he used for drag racing. He told Betnar that O'Hara was inside, waiting to talk to him.

Sitting outside, Plante could hear Betnar's screams while he was being beaten. The man emerged bleeding, with welts on his arms and face. He limped back to Plante's vehicle, whimpering.

Most of the Hells Angels' victims would have stayed quiet about a beating and life would have gone on as usual for members of the most powerful gang on the West Coast. But Betnar contacted police, who offered to put him into witness protection and relocate him. With Betnar's evidence, Plante was arrested and charged with extortion. O'Hara was also arrested and jointly charged with extortion**.

Plante was taken to jail in Surrey. After sitting in his cell for a few hours, he made a decision that would change his life forever.

---

* O'Hara has since left the Hells Angels and now works as a welding contractor.
** The charges against Plante and O'Hara were later dropped by the Crown.

He decided to call the RCMP detachment located next to the jail and tell them that he was willing to play ball with the police.

The fact that Plante was a trusted associate of the East End Hells Angels certainly caught the attention of police, who had been trying for years to find someone to infiltrate the gang. The police alleged the East End Hells Angels were well-known in the criminal underworld for controlling the cocaine trade at a wholesale level, using violence to persuade potential competition to stay away.

In recent years, the bikers had expanded into the production and distribution of synthetic drugs such as ecstasy and metham-phetamine, known on the street as crystal meth, as well as moving into Internet porn and online gambling, police claimed.

Plante was taken to an interview room where he was visited by two Mounties, who would eventually become his police "handlers." One of the officers in particular asked why he was willing to work with the police. The Mountie wanted to make sure Plante wasn't intending on playing the role of a double agent—undertaking counter surveillance of police and reporting back to his biker buddies. Plante gave the officer a quick synopsis of how he came to be where he was, and stressed he wasn't happy with the direction his life had taken.

The officer told Plante that, based on the witness statement relating to the extortion charges, the bouncer was looking at doing prison time. But Plante was told that if he was interested in cooperating, police could make the charges go away.

Plante told the cop he was interested but hesitant, knowing that people who cooperate with the police in Hells Angels investigations usually end up dead.

Well, think it over, the cop said. Here's my card. Give me a call if you change your mind.

After he was returned to his cell, Plante did just that. He ruminated on where life had taken him and where he was headed—to prison for at least a couple of years. He asked to make a call, ostensibly to phone his lawyer. Plante wanted to know a bit more about what the police had in mind.

"We'll provide some expense money and see how it goes," he was told by the police.

Plante realized that if he accepted, there was no going back. Life as he knew it would be over. He had heard the bikers talk about what happens to "rats," as police informers are known in the criminal underworld.

The only good rat is a dead rat, he had been told repeatedly.

• • •

Hell to Pay is the explosive story of the takedown of the Hells Angels in Vancouver, based on evidence submitted by the Crown at trial, wiretaps submitted as evidence, testimony given at trial and interviews with police and underworld characters. As police and the authorities came to realize, the Hells Angels are a powerful and formidable foe, and as Michael Plante came to realize, folks you just never want to double-cross.

CHAPTER 1

The Cops Snare a Rat

The RCMP were excited about the prospect of having an informer with insider knowledge of the Hells Angels in Vancouver. Police had repeatedly publicly stated that the Hells Angels were the number one organized crime target in B.C., and the East End chapter, as a gang, had to date been able to avoid prosecution, earning a reputation for being untouchable.

Once he was released on bail, Plante called a pager number and arranged to meet with the RCMP to discuss the details of his work as an informant. The Mounties, who code-named the operation Project E-Pandora, initially offered Plante $2,000 a month for any information he could provide about the bikers. The amount was soon increased to $3,000 a month.

Plante agreed, perhaps underestimating the stress that lay ahead. "I was trying to make up for things I had done," he would later recall when discussing why he agreed to infiltrate the Hells Angels.

Plante was to prove instrumental in aiding police to accomplish what they had largely failed to do to date. In 2004, the Hells Angels had been operating in B.C. for more than 20 years, earning a notorious reputation for drug dealing and the use of violence to enforce control over their territory. The police had little to show the public in terms of successful prosecutions, which undermined public confidence in their ability to enforce the law against the Hells Angels.

An investigation in 2004 by the *Vancouver Sun* found that more than 60 percent of cases against the Hells Angels, including serious charges of drug trafficking, extortion and assault, ended in acquittals or with the Crown dropping the charges—known officially as a stay of proceedings.

A prime example of a glaring failure was the case of the *Western Wind*, a fishing boat loaded with cocaine that had been tracked from Colombia. According to police intelligence, its destination was Vancouver Island. The captain, Philip John Stirling, had offered the cops information about a large-scale cocaine smuggling operation linked to the Nanaimo and East End chapters of the Hells Angels. Stirling wanted $1 million in reward money as well as witness protection for himself and his family. Police initially agreed to Stirling's requests, then backed off, deciding he wasn't trustworthy.

As the boat headed toward Canadian waters—with Hells Angels members caught on police surveillance waiting on a dock in Nanaimo for its arrival—the Mounties took their decision about Stirling and asked U.S. authorities to intercept the boat before it reached its destination.

Accordingly, on February 21, 2001, the U.S. Coast Guard intercepted the *Western Wind* and arrested the crew. Found hidden in a secret compartment was 2.5 tons of pure cocaine valued at $250 million. The incredible outcome of the story was that no one was ever charged because U.S. prosecutors reportedly could not prove the drugs were destined for the United States.

For a time, Stirling fought to have the seized boat returned to him, but he eventually abandoned his efforts, especially after his negotiations with the RCMP became public in U.S. court documents.

Five years later, police would catch Stirling again with another ship, the *MV Baku*, off the coast of Vancouver Island. The ship, which had been tracked from Halifax and through the Panama Canal, was found to have bales of marijuana worth $6.5 million. But Stirling was lucky again—the Crown dropped all charges just before Christmas 2006 against Stirling and four other men, including two who had been aboard the *Western Wind*. The charges were reportedly dropped because of problems with the search, initially conducted by the Department of Fisheries and Oceans.

Police would later allege that one of those suspected of being involved in the *Western Wind* shipment was long-time Hells Angels member David Francis (Gyrator) Giles, a former Sherbrooke, Quebec Hells Angel before moving to B.C. and joining the East End chapter. Giles was never charged in the *Western Wind* case, however. Police also alleged that the masterminds behind the shipment were members of the Montreal Mafia, with the Hells Angels in B.C. tasked to transport the drugs to Quebec.

Although fingers were later pointed at a senior RCMP officer in B.C. as a prime example of the Mounties' failure to step up to the plate and properly pay the money needed to crack the case, others admitted that the Mountie in charge of the operation suffered from a failure to trust a source.

The case of the *Western Wind* also became a sore point among other police agencies frustrated by the lack of coordination of the various police forces involved that could have led to a successful prosecution.

Another of the failed cases led to a 2006 wrongful dismissal lawsuit by a former senior anti-biker gang police officer, Allen Dalstrom. According to court documents filed by Dalstrom, the case promised to expose long-standing jealousies, infighting and evidence of a "turf war" between the Vancouver police and the RCMP during an attempted crackdown on the Hells Angels.

Dalstrom had been working for the Organized Crime Agency of B.C. (OCABC), a joint forces agency tasked with targeting organized crime groups, when he was fired by the agency's commanding officer, David Douglas, in 2004. Concerns were raised about Dalstrom's alleged mishandling of the multimillion-dollar Hells Angels investigation code-named Project Phoenix. The case involved members of the Hells Angels who were never prosecuted. His superiors were also upset over comments Dalstrom allegedly made to a Montreal journalist, Julian Sher, about a botched case.

In documents filed in court to support his legal action, Dalstrom claimed he had done nothing wrong and the case against the Hells Angels could have been prosecuted, but in fact had been derailed by infighting caused by the RCMP.

"Certain members of the senior management of the RCMP in British Columbia were opposed to the creation of the OCABC from its inception because the OCABC was given the mandate to carry out investigations that had previously been within the mandate of the RCMP," Dalstrom alleged in his statement of claim. "The RCMP in British Columbia sought to persuade the province to disband the OCABC and return the mandate for investigating organized crime to the RCMP."

The witness list for his trial included some of the RCMP's top provincial officers, among them deputy commissioner Gary Bass, then the highest-ranking Mountie in B.C., former deputy commissioner Bev Busson and former Vancouver police chief Jamie Graham.

But just as the trial began, it was abruptly adjourned to allow lawyers for both sides to work out a deal, quashing the possibility of potentially explosive testimony about the alleged long-simmering rivalry between the Mounties and Vancouver police. Dalstrom received an out-of-court settlement, reportedly exceeding $2 million.

• • •

About a month after the *Western Wind* was intercepted—and days after Stirling and his crew were released without charge by the United States—police in B.C. celebrated the first significant prosecution of Hells Angels members in B.C. Two full-patch members of the East End chapter of the Hells Angels, Ronaldo "Ronnie" Lising and Francisco Batista "Chico" Pires, were convicted in 2001 of cocaine trafficking.

The case, known as Project Nova, involved Robert Molsberry, a drug dealer and petty criminal who had been a doorman at a Vancouver strip club, the No. 5 Orange, located at the corner of Main Street and Powell on the edge of the Gastown district—and a block from the Vancouver police station at 312 Main.

Molsberry had initially complained in 1996 to members of the Vancouver police that he feared for his safety because Ronnie Lising, Chico Pires and others were after him over unpaid drug debts. Molsberry agreed to wear a "wire"—a transmitting listening device that allows police to record conversations—and act as a police agent. In return for his cooperation, he was given $1,000 by Vancouver police to pay off his drug debts and promised a monthly payment throughout the investigation, plus a cash payment at the conclusion of the court proceedings.

The total amount he received was $25,000. He was also promised entry into the witness protection program when the investigation wrapped up. Based on their agreement with Molsberry, the police successfully applied for a consent wiretap authorization under section 184.2 of the Criminal Code. The wiretap was approved by then-B.C. Supreme Court justice Wally Oppal, who would later become an appeal court judge and the attorney general of B.C.

A group of trusted officers were selected to work on the covert case, which was run out of the offices of the OCABC to try to limit the number of police who knew about the investigation.

Police targeted two strip clubs: the No. 5 Orange and the Marble Arch. Drug transactions took place outside the Hells Angels clubhouse in East Vancouver, in gas stations, restaurants and gyms. The cocaine was referred to in pager messages and over cell phones in code as "lunch," "dinner" and "beer."

At trial, Lising and Pires were found to be joint operators of a "wholesale" cocaine business that supplied the No. 5 Orange and Marble Arch strip bars; police recorded 36 deliveries of cocaine to "retail salesmen" in 1996 and 1997. The transactions were worth $47,000 at the "wholesale" level—a term used by police to describe the sale of larger quantities of drugs destined to be sold later at the "street" level.

With Lising and Pires sentenced to four and a half years in prison, the case was hailed by police as the first significant prosecution against the Hells Angels in B.C. Police cited the case an as an example of their ability to protect witnesses who work with police and testify against the Hells Angels, hoping to encourage others to come forward.

"It sends a message: We're here for your protection if you want to work with the police. It sends a message to other people in this group," the late sergeant Larry Butler of the Outlaw

Motorcycle Gang Unit told the *Vancouver Sun* at the time. Another lead investigator in the case, inspector Andy Richards, then with the OCABC, said of the Lising–Pires convictions: "It's a clear indication that law enforcement can effectively target the Hells Angels. The system can work."

As a footnote to the case, there was an act of intimidation against one of the federal Crowns, Ernie Froess, whose life was threatened by aspiring Hells Angel John Virgil Punko, then 34, at the Pacific Centre food court in downtown Vancouver, two blocks from the courthouse. Punko was later convicted of uttering threats, which obviously impressed his Hells Angels colleagues, who eventually made him a full-patch member of the East End chapter. He would go on to have many dealings with the newest police infiltrator, Michael Plante.

• • •

Michael Plante grew up in Burnaby, a suburb of Vancouver, and attended Cariboo Hill High School. After completing grade 12, he took university courses at nearby Douglas College. To make money, he entered competitive weightlifting and body building: at one time, he was about 250 pounds and could bench-press 400 pounds. Initial background checks by police found that Plante had only been in minor trouble with the law; once he had got into an argument at a local gym and ended up charged with assault.

He first worked as a bouncer at the North Burnaby Inn's bar, which at one time was managed by Hells Angels member Bob Green, who is now a Nomad. Plante then moved to Alberta for a year, working as a bouncer in a bar in Medicine Hat. On his return to B.C., Plante got a job at Costco for five years, loading trucks and living a straight life. During that time, Plante claimed he didn't associate with the Hells Angels because he didn't work in a bar.

But he eventually did obtain a job as a bouncer. He had met many Hells Angels over the years, working as a bouncer at Coconuts nightclub in Burnaby and the Dell Hotel in Surrey, a hotel frequented by bikers where Angels would stash cocaine in the ceiling of one of the hotel rooms upstairs. Plante recalled being asked one night to sit in that hotel room to make sure nothing happened to the hidden cache of drugs, until someone came to collect it. He did this a couple of times a month for a year for the bikers.

Eventually, another aspiring Hells Angel, Randy Potts, got him a job at the Marble Arch strip club in downtown Vancouver, another biker bar. When the Marble Arch closed, then-Hells Angels member Louie Robinson got Plante a job as a bouncer at the Cecil Hotel strip club, where he worked weekends, 15 hours a day, making about $10 an hour.

At the time, Robinson ran an agency that booked strippers into bars and nightclubs in Vancouver and across British Columbia. The Cecil was known as a bar where Hells Angels and other gang members would socialize over beer with friends and business associates.

"It was very gang friendly," Plante said of the Cecil in those days. "Not just to biker groups, but all gangs."

While working at the Cecil, his long-time buddy Potts began using Plante as a middleman in drug deals, getting him to pick up drugs and deliver them, or to pick up the cash and bring it to Potts. At the time, Potts had applied to become a Hells Angel and had reached hangaround status, meaning he could wear a leather vest with an insignia on the front indicating he was in a Hells Angels "program."

In 2003, Potts was beaten up by somebody who then stole his vest. He returned to the East End clubhouse with a black eye and informed Louie Robinson, who was at the time a senior member, of the incident.* Plante recalled hearing Potts being slapped by Robinson and Potts falling to the floor. Potts was told to "get rid of" the thief, named Audey Hanson, who had beaten him up, so Potts and Plante went to stake out his Surrey home; the stakeout continued over a two-month period.

Potts eventually gave Plante two guns—an Uzi sub-machine gun and a .38 handgun—and dropped him off at Hanson's house with orders to kill him. Plante recalled he purposefully jammed the Uzi and pointed it at Hanson when he came out of the house. Wearing a balaclava, Plante fired the .38 three times in the air to scare the man, who ran inside the house.

Plante told Potts the Uzi had jammed. "He didn't believe me," Plante recalled. Potts later gave the guns to another friend, who did shoot Hanson, who fortunately survived the murder attempt.

---

* Robinson is no longer a member of the Hells Angels.

CHAPTER 2

"I signed my life away..."

"There was no grudge for doing what I did," Plante would later explain. "The things they [the Hells Angels] were getting away with, I didn't think it was right." The new informant added that he was compelled by "moral and ethical reasons" to betray his biker colleagues. Probably no one will know how much of this sentiment was self-serving or really reflected the way he felt.

Plante was initially paid $2,000 a month by police to work as an informer and gather information about the activities of Hells Angels members in Vancouver. His classification as an informant meant that, while he was paid for information, his identity would be kept secret and he would not have to testify in court. At the outset of the relationship, police wanted to see how he would perform under stress and then decide how to proceed.

He had started off his career with the Hells Angels "middling"—that is, being the middleman in drug deals. The bouncer also helped to supply the prescription painkiller Percocet to Potts and another East End chapter biker, John Virgil Punko—both Randy Potts and Punko would later blame Plante for "feeding" their Percocet addictions.

By March 2004, Potts was actively engaged in the production and distribution of methamphetamine, relying on his criminal associate, Wissam (Sam) Ayach, for distribution. Because of a recent police bust, Potts needed to locate a new meth cook, so Plante introduced to him to Ryan Renaud, who knew how to produce the highly addictive street drug known as crystal meth.

On March 19 and 20, 2004, Plante acted as the go-between for Potts, transferring $14,000 and 36 pounds of ephedrine, an ingredient used to make crystal meth, to Renaud, who wanted the money to purchase hydriodic acid, another requirement in the production of crystal meth.

Then, in April 2004, the RCMP offered Plante a new contract that would make him a police agent. Becoming an agent would require him to testify in court should charges be laid based on any information supplied by him before he could collect reward money. This was a huge leap for Plante, and the deeper he got into the police investigation, with more Hells Angels added as targets, the more stressful his life became. The strain of leading a double life was compounded by his knowing that one wrong move could cost him his life.

There were compensations, however—police would eventually offer him $1 million in reward money—$500,000 at the end of the investigation, the rest after all the trials were finalized. He would also get more money a month—up to $14,000, plus expenses.

The deal also came with new restrictions—a police agent cannot break the law without the authorization of his police "handlers"—so any illegal activities he would have to undertake would have to be cleared ahead of time. If he was going to lay a beating on someone on behalf of the Hells Angels, he would have to phone the police first and get approval. His double life also meant that he had hardly any time for a private life, even with his girlfriend. The Hells Angels would call him at 2 a.m. and he would have to respond immediately to prove he wanted to become a full member of the club.

Plante immediately felt his stress level rising, imagining what might lie ahead and how complicated the restrictions would make things. He said he needed time to think about the offer. He read the agreement carefully but didn't sign it for six days. Once he signed, he knew there would be no going back.

"It was a big step. Really big," he recalled of signing the document. "I was signing my life away. The life I previously knew."

Plante soon realized working for police was more stressful than he expected. He constantly had to phone his handlers. In one such call, he said, "Potts is getting me to pick up a load of guns from his mom's house—what should I do?" Pick up the guns, meet us, let us have a look at them, then carry on, police said.

"Now I'm picking up crystal meth from a cook," he told his handlers. They instructed him to go to a nearby "safe house," an apartment rented by police located a few blocks from Plante's home in New Westminster. The drugs were then weighed and photographed by police before Plante delivered the shipment.

Almost daily, he was undertaking illegal activity for Hells Angels members. Dropping off a kilo of meth at a deli, picking up cash, arranging the next delivery of drugs. It was nerve-racking and terribly time-consuming. Plante had to meet with police often for debriefing sessions to discuss what was happening. Police would record the debrief conversations, taking detailed notes, which would be used in police affidavits to support judicial applications to wiretap Hells Angels members. His biker bosses, meanwhile, were also on his back, wanting to know why it was taking so long to make his deliveries.

. . .

On April 4, Renaud phoned Plante to say the first batch of meth was cooked and ready for pickup. The next day, Plante picked up 1.1 pounds of meth for Potts. A week later, Plante collected another 6.7 pounds from Benjamin Azernoul, an associate of the East End chapter and a runner for Renaud.* The hand-off of the drugs, a yellowish-white substance in five Ziploc bags placed inside a Timberland shoe box, occurred in the parking lot of the Canada Games pool in New Westminster, a suburb of Vancouver.

Plante planned to deliver the drugs to Potts but another Hells Angels member, John Punko, found out about it and wanted to use the 6.7 pounds of meth to finance his own cook with Renaud. At the time, Punko was a full-patch Hells Angels member while Potts was only a "prospect." Since Punko was the higher-ranking member, he had seniority and authority over both Plante and Potts. Punko told Plante to deliver three pounds of meth to the home of Sam Ayach, in Surrey, who sold drugs for the Hells Angels.

Potts and Plante showed up at Ayach's residence to talk to him at one point, but Ayach didn't answer his door. Potts and Plante walked inside to look for him and Plante found Ayach hiding in a closet, but didn't tell Potts.

Plante later returned alone to talk to Ayach, who agreed to take a kilo of methamphetamine on behalf of Potts and a kilo on behalf of Punko. Plante told Ayach to sell the kilo for Punko right

---

* Azernoul was charged with drug trafficking but the charges were eventually stayed by the Crown.

away, but to take his time selling Potts' meth—at least a month or two.

Three days later, Ayach gave Plante $13,000 for the sale of Punko's meth. At the time he picked up the money, Plante dropped off another kilo of the drug for Punko. Ayach gave Plante a $3,000 advance on Punko's second kilo. As instructed, Ayach confirmed he still hadn't sold Potts' meth.

On April 16, 2004, police advised Plante to stay away from Ayach's residence, where the RCMP executed a search warrant, seizing four pounds of methamphetamine. Ayach and his girlfriend were arrested and Ayach was kept in custody, ending his career as a crystal meth distributor for the bikers.

Three days after the Ayach bust, Punko met with Plante at a 7-Eleven store; then they went to Fitness Quest gym and later to a White Spot restaurant for a bite to eat.

"I hope my fuckin' name's not in there anywhere," Punko confided to Plante, referring to the search warrant executed on Ayach's residence. Plante told Punko police had seized four pounds of meth at Ayach's house—two pounds belonging to Punko, the other two to Potts.

Punko said he was going to "jump in the picture and lay on Randy [Potts] hard," accusing him of "going around Surrey with the bottom rocker on." This was a reference to Potts only having the "bottom rocker" insignia of the Hells Angels that said "British Columbia" and not the full patch, which included the winged Death's Head logo, and the top rocker, which says "Hells Angels."

Police refer to it as the "power of the patch." The three-piece patch identifies the wearer as a full member of the Hells Angels. Just seeing a member wearing the Hells Angels patch can strike fear into low-level criminals with no gang affiliation to protect them. Infamous Hells Angels member Sonny Barger referred to the club as "one on all, all on one," meaning when a person fights with one Hells Angel, he fights with all Hells Angels. Their power extends to clubs around the world, making it difficult to escape the wrath of the Angels.

Plante asked Punko if he wanted to give the two remaining pounds of meth to Renaud so he could sell them. "Yeah, yeah, let's give it to him," the biker replied.

Plante explained the meth cook still owed Punko $10,000, which Punko suggested could be used for another meth cook. Punko suggested getting a half barrel of ephedrine, one of the primary ingredients in meth production. Plante explained a half barrel cost about $80,000 and a full barrel was about $160,000.

Punko swore that Renaud was "gonna get fuckin' pounded right out" if he didn't produce. The biker also expressed concern about the police heat around the Ayach bust and warned Plante to be extra careful dealing with the cook.

"I'm getting nervous—don't wanna get busted here," Punko explained as the police wiretap picked up. "That's why we gotta get those phones activated tomorrow for sure," the biker instructed, suggesting to Plante they use new "clean" cell phones that couldn't be traced to them.

Punko also discussed getting some dynamite from a Surrey acquaintance, whose initials were R.T. Plante asked Punko what he would use the explosives for. "Ya never know, man," Punko replied. "We're in the Hells Angels. It's a vicious biker club. You never know."

The next day, Punko and Plante met at the home of R.T. After the meeting, Plante suggested, "It's time to fill up that fuckin' shoe box, man." Punko added he wouldn't mind having a meeting with the meth cook, Renaud.

On April 21, 2004, Plante met with Punko at the tennis courts on Burnaby Mountain, a place that Punko felt would be free of police listening devices, allowing the two men to speak freely.

Later, Punko and Plante went to a coffee shop on East Hastings, where Plante explained a meeting was scheduled with the meth cook that night. Punko said he wanted to tell Renaud that he couldn't cook for anyone else.

"Just partners all the way, you tell him not to do nobody else's shit. That's it, you stop, fuckin', you stop right now."

Renaud met Plante and Punko in the parking lot of Fitness Quest gym in New Westminster. Punko stressed they were all playing on the same team. He also wanted Renaud to make sure his partner in the cook, Dave Pearse, got that message. "Make sure you tell Dave," Punko explained. "You got a [Hells Angels] member on the other end that's fuckin' willing to do anything for you two guys. Just fuckin' make sure, fuckin' be smart, be honest and fuckin' make money, an' that's it."

Punko also warned Renaud to tell Pearse not to "name drop" about whom they were working for. He didn't want the meth cook and his buddy going around blabbing about cooking for a Hells Angel. The biker also said he wanted to meet Pearse to "let Dave know who the fuck I am, okay?"

Plante slapped and shoved Renaud at one point. He later explained he was playing the "bad cop" role while Punko played the "good cop" in order to drive home the message not to fuck around with a Hells Angels member. Plante also wanted to reassure Punko that he could take care of his business for him.

The discussion then turned to business—the ingredients that needed to be purchased and how much money was required. Renaud said they would need to invest $35,000 each in the meth cook, which would include a half barrel of ephedrine. The return on investment would be 12.5 kilos, which, at $13,000 a kilo, would be worth almost $165,000, for a profit of $23,000 each, Renaud explained.

Renaud gave Plante a handwritten note that itemized the costs of ingredients and production expenses that included $3,500 for liquid, $1,200 for color, $1,200 for Red Bull—the caffeinated drink that would allow the cooks to stay awake during long hours of working—and $3,000 for renting the space for the lab.

· · ·

After the meeting with Renaud, Plante went to the East End Hells Angels clubhouse, located at 3598 East Georgia Street, near the eastern boundary of Vancouver and the adjacent suburb of Burnaby, where some Hells Angels ran legitimate businesses—Damiano Dipopolo ran Digstown Clothing at the time, for example, and across the street was the Big Shots coffee bar, whose director at the time was listed as Francisco Pires.

Punko arrived at the clubhouse a minute later and wanted to talk about Renaud. They got in Punko's vehicle and began driving, with Plante's wire allowing police to record the conversation.

Plante told Punko he had picked up a box of money from Renaud—an orange Nike shoe box containing $45,550 cash in bundles of Canadian bills in 10s, 20s, 50s and 100s. Police would later photograph the contents of the box and give it back to Plante. Plante told Punko he needed to take out $20,000 and "give it to Putzhead," a reference to Potts.

"Twenty out of that, eh?" Punko responded.

"Yeah, it fuckin' sucks, eh?" Plante said. "Well, that's the way we're going to do it, right? We're just gonna take a little bit out, just to keep us goin' an' then just keep rollin' over, right?"

"Right," Punko responded.

"We don't have to slum," Plante added. "He just takes it an' goes. Know what I mean?"

"But I've got a fuckin' strange feelin' we're gonna get ripped off, man," Punko said.

"We just made fuckin', you know, sixty Gs, fuck. What did we do? Nothing," Plante observed, referring to the $16,000 from Ayach and the box of cash from Renaud.

About two weeks later, sergeant Dan Russell, one of the lead investigators on Project E-Pandora, was advised by Surrey RCMP that further arrests were expected—police planned to arrest Plante, Potts and Punko "all for meth as a result of information."

Russell advised the head of the E-Pandora investigation, then-inspector Bob Paulson, of this development. Paulson contacted inspector Collins at the Surrey detachment, explaining that the planned arrests could jeopardize their ongoing investigation. Collins agreed Surrey RCMP would not arrest Potts, Punko and Plante.

Days later, Plante found another trafficker, Chad Barroby, who would buy two pounds of the meth, which Plante delivered.

About a week later, Potts showed Plante a list of very expensive lab equipment—Plante estimated it would cost $300,000—that could be used to produce meth. Plante knew Potts didn't have the wherewithal to make the purchase.

From the beginning, Potts was addicted to the prescription drug Percocet, a painkiller, which Plante supplied to the biker with the consent of police. It made Potts erratic and unpredictable at times.

Later that night, at about 8 p.m., Punko and Plante met at Fitness Quest gym in New Westminster. Also there were Renaud and Nima Ghavami, a bouncer who worked with Plante at the Cecil Hotel strip club. Punko and Plante later went to Punko's nearby home, where Plante showed Punko the list of lab equipment Potts had provided earlier.

Punko told Plante that Renaud was going to be "Punko's cook" and he didn't want him cooking for anyone else. "I'm going to freak on Ryan [Renaud] when I see him next time. I'm going to tell him, 'Stay the fuck out' or I'll smash his face in." Partly it was the Percocet addiction talking, Plante thought.

Punko also warned Plante to be aware that police were probably following him.

"Listen, you're a friend of the club," Punko advised. "You don't think these guys are on your ass? The cops are around us all the time." The biker added: "We're in a biker club, man. It's fuckin' more serious than you think."

He went on to say, "One of us gets brought down, we all get brought down. You get brought down, you bring me down too."

Punko suggested they needed to have a meeting with Renaud "at the right place, the right time" and "lay down the law" with him. The partnership would be Punko, Plante, Renaud and Pearse. "Nobody else. They work for us," Punko reiterated.

After they had cooked half a barrel, Punko wanted to roll over the profits and do a full barrel "and do it again." Later, Punko would declare: "We need a money machine. We're getting big time now, man."

• • •

On May 26, 2004, Plante had an undisclosed disagreement with then-corporal Gary Shinkaruk and walked out of a meeting in a huff after Shinkaruk told him, "It's not working out."

Shinkaruk advised another officer after the meeting that he was of the opinion that Plante "no longer wanted to cooperate with the investigation."

Three days later, Shinkaruk had a phone conversation with Plante, who was still steamed. He told Shinkaruk he would not deal with him, that Shinkaruk could "take the motorcycle back" and settle up any outstanding finances the RCMP owed. Plante was so angry that at one point he threatened to punch Shinkaruk in the head if he saw him. The Mountie hung up on Plante.

After Plante cooled down, he called Shinkaruk later that night and apologized for getting so wound up. Shinkaruk told Plante that he needed to meet with him to debrief him on his actions over the past few days and to discuss the requirements for Plante to continue as a police agent.

Plante also signed new one-party consent forms for interception of his private communications and for surveillance to be undertaken by video. The investigation and wiretap operation then resumed.

. . .

About three weeks after Plante's first meth delivery to Barroby, Plante met him again at a 7-Eleven store. Barroby handed over $10,000, which was partial payment for the previous two pounds of meth. Plante handed the money over to Potts.

On June 8, 2004, police decided to buy the remaining 14 pounds of meth Plante was holding for Potts, waiting to find buyers. Police told Plante to use a ruse—to tell Potts he had found a buyer in Alberta willing to pay $11,500 a pound. Potts offered to pay Plante $500 a pound for making the sale, adding, "Are you sure that's enough for you?"

Plante gave Potts $22,000 later that month—the first payment from the sales to the Alberta buyer.

"I love ya, buddy," Potts responded, clearly pleased to be getting a chunk of cash. "Twelve more to go," he added, referring to the fact that there were still 12 more pounds waiting to be sold, which showed that Potts was unaware that Punko had ripped off 6.7 pounds.

"Load him up," Potts told Plante, meaning keep the drugs flowing to the Alberta buyer.

"Just keep going?" Plante asked. Potts was so pleased he suggested Plante should "give a break" on the price to the Alberta buyer.

Punko also met with Renaud at Punko's house. They discussed how Punko wanted to reinvest the profits from the first cook and do a full barrel next time. "Do I need to meet Dave [Pearse] or not?" Punko asked Renaud at one point. "Because he knows who we are, eh?"

"Yeah," Renaud replied. "It's all good."

• • •

Later in June, Plante was surprised to learn police were planning to bust Renaud's meth lab in Abbotsford. The police agent learned of the impending raid during a meeting with police one night at the underground parking lot of the safe house.

Plante made it clear to his handlers that it was a stupid idea. He argued that Renaud was key to Plante's ability to collect evidence against Potts and Punko. He opposed any police action that would lead to Renaud's arrest.

"Without him, there's nothing," Plante explained to his handlers.

Police suggested Punko would adapt and find another meth cook.

"How?" Plante replied, his temper flaring. "I got nothin' else. You took away Sammy [Ayach] and then take away Ryan [Renaud], then there's nothin' else. There's fuck all—I got nothin'... Randy [Potts] has nothin' and it'll put a scare into all of them and they'll all disappear."

Police ignored Plante's protests and Renaud's drug lab at 6521 Little Street in Abbotsford was raided by police on June

25, 2004. The lab was located in an outbuilding on a farm. Lab equipment was seized but no methamphetamine was found by police—Renaud had moved nine buckets of crystal meth to another location just before the raid.

The next day, Plante met with Renaud for more than an hour to discuss the setback. Plante then went to Punko's residence to relay his conversation with Renaud about the bust.

On June 27, Punko and Plante both met with Renaud to discuss the next step. After Renaud left, Punko expressed concern about Renaud being busted, saying Renaud had the potential to make a lot of money for Punko. The biker mused that he wanted to get Renaud out of town somewhere and set him up in a meth lab that wouldn't attract police attention.

Plante and Potts continued selling the meth they had on hand. Plante bought another two pounds of meth from Potts on July 13, 2004, paying Potts $21,000, with cash provided by Plante's RCMP handlers.

Two weeks later, his handlers told him to buy another three pounds for $31,500 cash. During the sale, Plante told Potts: "We'll be back, uh, probably next weekend and I'll load 'em up again."

"Rock and roll," Potts replied, obviously happy about the wads of cash rolling in. During the meeting, Plante also agreed to give Potts an injection of steroids—injected into Potts' buttocks.

Three days later, Ghavami delivered $45,000 to Plante at the Fitness Quest gym. The money was from Renaud, with Ghavami allegedly acting as the go-between.

Later that night, Plante met his handlers at the safe house, where police counted the money, which was in a plastic bag. It was supposed to be nine bundles of $5,000 but was $200 short. The handlers told Plante to deliver $25,000 cash to Punko. Plante told Punko that Renaud still owed them $10,000 each to account for the shortfall.

Punko again stressed he needed to get Renaud out of town, to set up a drug lab in a remote house somewhere in the interior of B.C. "Once we get this fuckin' house and get the guy up there, he ain't leavin', man. He's staying there," Punko explained. "And I'll read him the riot act."

Punko also suggested he was going to cut Renaud's partner, Dave Pearse, out of the lab. But Plante pointed out that Pearse was the one with all the lab equipment. "So Dave's gonna be our fourth partner here, eh?" Punko said, accepting the fact that they needed lab equipment to continue the operation.

Plante later met Renaud at Fitness Quest gym, telling him that Punko planned to buy a house in the interior for the meth lab. While Punko was out of town for a few days to look at houses, Plante met with Renaud and Pearse in the lot of the Carter Dodge Chrysler dealership at 4650 Lougheed Highway in Burnaby. While pretending to look at new cars, they discussed how they were going to handle "ripping off" a barrel of ephedrine from a man referred to as "Sam the Hindu."

Punko returned to town on July 25, 2004, informing Plante he had looked at a number of houses for a new meth lab. Plante advised him that there was already meth in production again.

Punko stated he wanted to make "a million bucks" from the operation and advised Plante to "lean on him [Renaud] hard" to keep producing. A few days later, Punko was getting worked up again about Renaud, telling Plante: "I'm gonna fuckin' rip that little goof's face off."

"Why, what happened?" Plante asked.

Punko ducked the question. "Nothing," he replied. "I'll fuckin' smash his hands and he won't be able to work."

The next day, August 2, 2004, Plante met with Renaud outside the Gibson Kickboxing gym in Port Moody, a suburb east of Vancouver. Renaud gave Plante $9,000 as an advance on the future proceeds of a kilogram of meth held by drug dealer Jay Brown, who had been arrested and was in custody, with the drugs still in Brown's apartment.

Renaud explained in a note he wrote for Punko that he was getting out of town for two weeks. "Sorry I couldn't meet—had to leave," the note said. "We'll pick up where we left off when I'm back." Renaud estimated it would take two weeks to cook up another batch of meth.

Plante later met with his RCMP handlers, who counted and photographed the latest cash delivery. The RCMP instructed him to deliver the $9,000, along with Renaud's note, to Punko. Plante met Punko in a Costco parking lot in Burnaby. Punko took the cash and read Renaud's note.

"I'm gonna fuckin' slap that fuckin' Ryan," Punko reacted, upset that Renaud had left town without checking with him first. "I'm going to freak on him, but I'm tellin' ya, I'm fuckin' ready to blow up, man." The biker instructed Plante to buy two new cell phones the next day. Punko then left, still steamed.

"He better have the ingredients, 'cause if he don't, we'll have to go fuckin' scout around," Punko said as he was leaving, referring to Renaud having all the chemicals needed for the next meth cook.

• • •

In August 2004, Plante arranged to meet full-patch member Ronaldo "Ronnie" Lising at a Chinese restaurant, the Gourmet Castle, on East Hastings in Vancouver. During the meeting, Lising used a hand signal—turning a key—to indicate to Plante that he wanted to buy a kilo.

"Coke?" Plante asked.

"No, the other stuff," Lising replied, instructing Plante to take the kilo to a deli, which was then owned by Lising's brother.* Lising gave instructions on how to get to the deli, which was located at Champlain Mall in Burnaby.

Lising also advised Plante not to wear Hells Angels support wear when he made the delivery to avoid attracting police attention. "Don't look so 'heaty,'" Lising said, meaning Plante shouldn't wear anything with as Hells Angels insignia, which might attract the "heat" of police attention.

An undercover police surveillance team watched as Plante delivered the kilo of methamphetamine to the deli.

Days later, Punko was upset when he heard that Renaud had been talked to by Lising. Punko said if Renaud "fucks up, I'll shatter his hand so bad he won't be able to stir nothin'."

On August 10, 2004, Plante phoned Punko, advising he was going to be out of town for a week with Ghavami for a short vacation.

When Plante returned, Punko called to talk about Renaud, who by then had a new residence in New Westminster. The next day, Plante met with Renaud at his house. The meth cook said he had already produced two kilograms and the rest would be done by the end of the week. He estimated Punko and Plante would each get about $40,000 after expenses.

Plante took Renaud over to Punko's house so the biker could hear the good news first hand. Punko seemed pleased but continued talking about his plan to buy a house out of town, where Renaud would cook exclusively for Punko, without distractions or access to anyone else.

Plante, meanwhile, was still feeling tense about Punko ripping off almost seven kilograms of the meth that belonged to Potts. It

---

* Lising's brother was never charged.

was eating away at him, knowing he couldn't stall Potts forever. But he knew he had to obey Punko, who was a full-patch member.

He discussed the rip-off with his handlers, who decided to see what they could do to ease Plante's stress. On August 23, 2004, the RCMP gave Plante $42,000, which he used to pay Potts for another fictitious "sale" of meth, this time for four pounds. Plante gave Potts the cash in the parking lot of Woody's Pub in Coquitlam. Potts was wearing his Hells Angels "prospect" vest, with the bottom rocker on the back. Potts drove off in his black Hummer.

Plante was later given another $25,000 by the RCMP, which he gave to Potts, to cover for the remaining 2.7 pounds ripped off by Punko. When Plante gave Potts his final payment, he told the biker that the Alberta buyer was looking to buy more but Renaud "was in the middle of the thing right now" and consequently couldn't start a new cook.

He didn't dare tell Potts that Renaud was now cooking for Punko. Instead, they discussed moving some cocaine.

"I asked him [Potts] something about those 30 ounces of cocaine that he has," Plante explained to his handlers, adding that Potts said he had them stored at the home of someone named C.J.

One of the handlers asked Plante how much Potts wanted for the coke. Plante replied $1,000 an ounce, even though ounces were selling on the street for $800 to $900. Plante explained Potts was "stuck in the 1980s and that's why he has no customers." He meant Potts' prices were too high because a glut of cocaine on the streets had forced down the price.

Inspector Shinkaruk told Plante that if the word got out that Plante was looking for some coke "then some other guys will want you to get some coke."

The initial police plan was to use Potts and Punko to get at other, more senior "targets" within the East End Hells Angels.

The RCMP gave Plante $4,800 to buy four ounces of cocaine from Potts, figuring the high price offered might bring others sellers to Plante.

Plante, however, felt he wasn't getting anywhere with Potts and Punko and the rest of the East End chapter. He repeatedly asked police if he could target the Nomads chapter because it seemed to be where all the action was.

Plante called Potts and Punko "two mopes" and referred to the rest of the East End chapter as the "geriatric crew" and a "bunch of old jokers . . . a bunch of broken-down bums," complaining they were stuck in the past. The East End members, he said, were afraid of the rising United Nations gang, a multiethnic gang that was growing in strength and numbers.

The UN mainly controlled the drug trade in the Fraser Valley, shipping B.C. Bud—potent, high-grade hydroponic marijuana—across the border in exchange for cocaine and guns. The gang had made a name for itself by not being afraid to stand up to and fight with the Hells Angels.

Plante explained to his handlers that the East End Hells Angels members were "scared of what happened in Quebec," a reference to the street battle for turf that broke out in Montreal between the Hells Angels and the rival Rock Machine, which left more than 100 dead and led to a sweeping crackdown by Quebec police.

Despite telling police they were wasting their time pursuing East End Hells Angels, Plante failed to convince police that he should switch over to infiltrating the Nomads. He was told the police were adamant about nailing two long-time members of the East End chapter—Louie Robinson and David Giles.

In addition, police were not convinced Plante was established enough to be trusted by the Nomads. They hoped he would rise through the Hells Angels "program," become a member and then try to infiltrate the Nomads.

Plante met with Renaud again on September 1, 2004, in the parking lot of Fitness Quest gym in New Westminster. The meth cook explained the total revenue from sales of the last meth cook had come to $162,000. The cook gave Plante a detailed list of total expenses, which came to $34,500. Some of the meth had been sold for $13,000 a kilo and others fetched $14,000, Renaud said, adding that Plante and Punko should each set aside $7,000 to reinvest in the next meth cook.

Renaud gave Plante $56,000 as profit, with $34,000 for Punko. Plante's share came to $21,500, Renaud explained, because he had given Ghavami a kilogram of meth, which he was holding for Plante.

Plante was already feeling pangs of guilt about getting Ghavami involved in the drug business. Ghavami was his friend, not a target, but Ghavami was being seduced into the drug trade by the money he saw flowing. Still, he knew he had to tell police. One of the conditions of his agreement was to tell the truth and not to hide anything.

Plante met with his handlers in the parking lot of the safe house. He took two plastic bags from the trunk of his car—one containing $34,000 cash, the other containing $21,500. Police took photos of the bags and their contents, then kept Plante's share of the money. They instructed him to carry on and give Punko his cash.

Later that day, Plante went to the East End chapter clubhouse, where members were gathered for a weekly meeting, known as "church." After the meeting, Punko invited Plante upstairs, where they sat down to discuss the breakdown of expenses and profits from the meth cook. Plante left the clubhouse at about 10 p.m. and drove to Punko's house, giving the biker his bag of profits.

"Hey, see this?" Punko said, motioning to the cash. "We should be havin' stacks like that, man." Punko told Plante he wanted to use a full barrel for the next cook.

• • •

Three weeks later, Plante met Punko at the King Sushi restaurant in New Westminster to discuss reinvesting money with Renaud. Punko told Plante to "stand on this guy," meaning Renaud.

Later that evening, Plante went to Punko's home and collected $6,800, which was Punko's share of the investment in Renaud's next cook. It was supposed to be $7,000 but Punko was $200 short. Plante later met with his handlers, who photographed the money, which was all in $20 bills.

Two days later, Plante met with Renaud at the gym. Plante handed over Punko's money, plus Plante's $8,000 share, provided by the RCMP, for the next meth cook.

About a month later, Plante and Renaud went to Punko's house for a meeting. Punko grilled Renaud, saying he had heard Renaud had a relationship with Clay Roueche, the leader of the UN gang, rivals of the Hells Angels. Punko wanted to know whose side Renaud was on—"ours or theirs?"—and about the current state of meth production.

"I want this money, man," Punko demanded of Renaud. "Fuckin' let's be greedy about it. Because one fuckin' day soon—it could take five years, it could be ten years, it could be two weeks—it's going to stop, man, so you've gotta make it now when you can."

After the meeting with Renaud, Punko suggested he needed to make a quick $20,000 and asked Plante how he could make that happen. They discussed selling five kilograms of cocaine to Plante's Alberta buyer. Punko agreed, but warned Plante not to mention the cocaine deal to Jonathan Bryce Jr. "If you say five, I can get it for sure," Punko explained to Plante, referring to five kilos of cocaine.

Days later, Plante received $30,000 from the RCMP as a down payment on the five kilograms of cocaine, which were priced at $25,000 a kilo. When Plante arrived at Punko's house with the money, the biker bragged the coke was "the best around."

Punko asked how much Plante was selling the kilos for in Alberta. "Thirty," Plante replied, referring to $30,000. Punko figured they would each make $12,500 profit on the deal.

After Plante dropped off the money, Punko drove to the nearby Kensington Mall parking lot, where a Jeep Liberty pulled in. Both vehicles drove away in tandem and arrived at Punko's house, where an undercover police surveillance team observed Punko remove two gym bags from his vehicle.

The next day, Plante picked up the five kilos at Punko's house. Punko said he got the cocaine from "R.T. and this Chinese guy." Police later tested the bricks of cocaine and found the purity was between 82 percent and 84 percent, indicating it was from a source country such as Colombia.

Plante, after making his fictitious sale to his buyer in Alberta, later delivered the rest of the cash owing to Punko, plus a split of the profits.

In the meantime, Renaud had another meth cook in the works and Plante discussed selling the meth in Alberta for $20,000 a kilo. More meth profits were delivered to Punko, who confided he stashed his cash at his brother's house in Burnaby.* With four more barrels, Punko said, we'll make $1 million cash.

"Let's do it—this is where the money is," Punko said. "Let's not stop now, man, but just focus."

---

* The brother was never charged.

On October 21, 2004, Plante had a long talk with Potts, who was again short of money. Potts said he still had 26 ounces of cocaine for sale, adding he had paid just under $1,000 an ounce. Plante suggested he could sell the cocaine to his Alberta buyer, which would result in Potts getting $2,000 profit.

"That would help," Potts said.

The conversation then shifted to methamphetamine—Plante said Renaud was just finishing a cook and needed a barrel of ephedrine, which cost about $160,000, before he could start another cook. Potts asked Plante if he was producing meth with Renaud.

"I just reinvest my money," explained Plante, bragging about how much money he was making. Potts complained he hadn't made any money in about eight months. He wanted to do another half barrel and asked Plante to make it happen. Plante sympathized, adding his Alberta connection was also broke and couldn't afford meth, so was looking for some coke to sell to make some money.

A week later, Plante picked up Potts' 26 ounces of cocaine and paid the biker $28,000, supplied by the RCMP. Only a day later, Potts told Plante he didn't have much money left.

"Is there any money available out there for me to borrow for a couple of weeks?" Potts asked, explaining he was short the money needed for the meth cook.

"You're not fuckin' gonna starve, trust me," Plante told him.

"Yeah, but I like to pay my end," Potts replied.

Plante suggested Potts could pay what he had—$60,000—and could owe the rest for the meth cook.

Renaud, however, was unable to do another meth cook just then. In order to maintain Plante's image as a successful producer, the RCMP got Plante to pretend the cook was happening and the Alberta buyer was again buying meth, allowing Plante to pay profits to Potts in installments. Again, the goal of the police was to use Potts to ensnare other East End members.

Plante met with Renaud and told him that another meth lab was doing a cook for Potts, who had only invested $60,000. He asked Renaud what kind of profit Potts should be paid. Renaud explained that a half barrel of ephedrine should produce 12.5 kilograms of meth, so the profit should be $21,000. But he suggested Plante hold back four kilos for all the expenses and the money Potts owed him.

Plante then told Potts he was going to Alberta to unload all of the meth. On New Year's Eve, 2004, Plante paid Potts $20,000 as partial payment for the fictitious meth sale. Days later, he paid Potts the rest of the profits—$66,000.

Plante was getting frustrated, realizing Potts didn't have the wherewithal to become a high-level drug dealer. He had to find another target. His final drug transaction with Potts occurred January 4, 2005, when he gave the biker his final $22,000 share of the last meth deal. He was getting fed up with Potts, whose addiction to painkillers was making the biker unfocused.

CHAPTER 3

An Official Friend

After Plante had gained the trust of many of the East End members, a senior biker suggested he should apply to join the Hells Angels. His police handlers were, of course, thrilled at the prospect of having someone on their payroll working inside the Hells Angels, but Plante realized it was going to mean more anxiety in his life. And he would soon learn how much money was expected to come out of his own pocket to become a Hells Angels member.

Once he became an "official friend" of the Hells Angels, it became Plante's responsibility to restock the East End Hells Angels' clubhouse bar each morning by 10 a.m. After a night of heavy partying by the bikers, this could easily cost him several hundred dollars, which he was expected to pay himself. He also had to provide security during weekly meetings.

Plante told his handlers about this new development, and they agreed to cover his added expenses. The Mounties also agreed to lease a Harley-Davidson motorcycle for Plante and pay for the lessons he needed to learn to ride it. They also bought him a 1997 Mustang to bolster his image as a successful drug dealer.

Plante became an official friend of the East End Hells Angels on September 22, 2004. He was called into a meeting room of the clubhouse by senior Hells Angels member David Giles. He was asked questions by the club president, John Bryce and other full-patch members including Giles, Lloyd Robinson and Joseph Bruce Skreptak.

The entire process took about 10 minutes. Plante had his photo taken, as did the others who were accepted as official friends at the same time: Bryce's son, Jonathan Bryce Jr., and Norm Cox.

The same evening, five full-patch Hells Angels—Ronaldo Lising, George Pires, his brother Chico Pires, Carlo Fabiano and Robert Alvarez—left the East End chapter for the Nomads chapter, which had a clubhouse nearby in Burnaby.

The Nomads are considered an elite chapter of the Hells Angels because, unlike the East End chapter whose territory is limited to East Vancouver, Nomads are not confined to a single territory. They can roam at will to do business, which police allege is mainly drug trafficking and violence to collect money or to punish perceived misdeeds. The ultimate punishment, of course, is death.

• • •

The Hells Angels are referred to by police as an "outlaw" motorcycle gang, which means they do not abide by society's rules. This doesn't mean, however, that the club itself doesn't have rules, and in fact, a long list of rules exists which each chapter must follow.

AN OFFICIAL FRIEND   43

To join the Hells Angels, you have to have a driver's licence, a motorcycle (a big Harley-Davidson, not a "sissy" bike) and have known a Hells Angels member for at least five years, which is how long Plante had known Randy Potts. Prospective Hells Angels members must also be male, white and cannot ever have applied for a job as a prison guard or a cop. "Snitches" or "rats"—people who rat out Angels to police—are prohibited, as are convicted rapists and child molesters. The Hells Angels also has unwritten rules: no criminal activity, which could draw the attention of the police, is permitted in the clubhouse and members should not disgrace the club by bringing attention to themselves.

Retired RCMP staff sergeant Jacques Lemieux, an expert on bikers and biker gangs from Quebec, often testified at B.C. Hells Angels trials that the main focus of the outlaw gang is drug trafficking. Chapters are established to control territory relating to trafficking (as well as other illegal activity) and are part of a sophisticated drug distribution network that relies on extensive and far-reaching connections in the criminal underworld.

One Vancouver trial heard testimony that police had seized six tons of hashish, which they hailed as a major bust. What investigators didn't realize at the time was that they had caught only the tail end of a 40-ton shipment that was one transaction of a US$165-million-a-year drug empire run by Claude Duboc, who shipped the "product" from Pakistan and for years used B.C. to offload from mother ships. Duboc was arrested in a $9,000-a-night hotel room in Hong Kong.

Police later learned that there were a further 20 tons of hash stashed in another warehouse. When Duboc's underlings were released on bail, they used the Hells Angels to ship the black hash across the country to Quebec, where it was sold for US$2.8 million per ton.

This was that kind of drug money that helped B.C. Hells Angels buy luxury homes and start legitimate businesses.

• • •

Enormous drug deals like this are a long way from the humble origins of the Hells Angels Motorcycle Club, often reduced to the acronym HAMC, which was started in California in 1948. Hells Angels is now an incorporated entity with its business address in Oakland, California. The Oakland chapter is considered the "mother" chapter, meaning that it must approve all matters concerning the club, including discipline, territorial disputes, the formation of new chapters and the acceptance of new members.

The Oakland chapter owns the copyright to the Death's Head logo and requires each Hells Angels member to pay $20 a year to wear the Hells Angels "colors." The club colors comprise red letters on a white background—hence the name the Red and White, which is often used to refer to the Hells Angels.

The club also uses the number 81, which stands for HA—H being the eighth letter of the alphabet, and A the first. For example, one B.C. Hells Angels member had owned a company called 81 Transport, which transported equipment for Vancouver's booming film industry. Despite its Hells Angels affiliation, the company is in demand, apparently because it provides good service to its customers.

The first step in the Hells Angels multi-level "program" to achieving full membership is to become an "official friend." The proposal that someone become an official friend must be voted on by chapter members and receive majority approval. Members at this lowest rank begin by guarding and maintaining the clubhouse, washing motorcycles and doing menial jobs for everyone ranking above them. Low-level aspiring Hells Angels are essentially gofers. They are at the beck and call of Hells Angels members, running errands, picking up supplies, even picking up members' children from school. Official friends cannot attend club meetings but provide security at meetings, which is known as "attending church."

The next level of membership is to become a "hangaround," which is self-explanatory. They get to hang around the clubhouse, tend the club bar and restock the booze supply and run errands. After that, the person becomes a "prospect," and they are given the "bottom rocker" which is the crest sewn on the bottom of the back of the Hells Angels vest. The bottom rocker for East End members says "British Columbia." On the front of the vest, a prospect has a small rectangular insignia, known as a flasher, that says "Prospect," as well as a flasher on the other side of the vest front saying "East End."

To become a full member, the candidate must receive unanimous approval in a vote of chapter members. Before the vote, the person's photograph is distributed to all Hells Angels members in the region, in case someone recognizes the candidate as a police operative or has ever had a run-in with him.

Once approved as a full-patch member, the biker receives the Hells Angels Death's Head insignia which is worn on the back of vests, along with the top rocker, which says Hells Angels and "MC," for motorcycle club, completing what is known as the patch or colors worn by full members. Some Hells Angels wear small patches on the front of their vests that say "Filthy Few," which police say is worn by those who have committed murder. Another small rectangular patch is the "Dequillo," which signifies that the Hells Angels fought the police when arrested.

The Death's Head insignia is a copyrighted logo owned by the Hells Angels. It is the club's property, not the member's, so when someone leaves the club, the colors have to be handed back to the club. Even when a Hells Angel dies, a club representative is dispatched to retrieve the deceased member's vest. Sometimes, if a member has a falling-out with the club, club tattoos will be removed by cutting the skin or using a blowtorch.

"Bearing the insignia of the club allows members to be identified as belonging to the most powerful outlaw biker gang in the world," RCMP biker expert Jacques Lemieux wrote in a 2004 report filed in court in support of police executing a search warrant at the Hells Angels clubhouse in Nanaimo, a chapter on Vancouver Island.

"It demands respect from other biker gangs and demonstrates the member's loyalty to the club," the report said. "The Hells Angels also wear their colors in order to intimidate other biker gangs and the general public, either directly or indirectly. Colors are sacred and only full club members can wear them. Prospects can only wear the lower rocker indicating the territory controlled by the club and the letters MC."

It can take three to four years for members to earn their patches. This, along with the fact that the Hells Angels has a structured hierarchy, makes it almost impossible for police to infiltrate the club.

Another police category of biker that doesn't have official status within the Hells Angels are "associates," who are trusted friends of Hells Angels members who don't attend weekly meetings but may be invited to club parties or on motorcycle "runs." Members are required to take part in annual motorcycle runs with fellow chapter members, which police say are used to mark territory. They are usually just party weekends with friends.

"The associate assists club members by facilitating, promoting and protecting their criminal activities," Lemieux stated in his report. Lemieux pointed out that Hells Angels use "puppet clubs"—biker gangs who are not Hells Angels but can wear their support wear, such as T-shirts and jackets with East End insignia, to intimidate others and let people know they are sanctioned by a particular chapter. Wearing support wear sends a message to other criminal groups that the person has a connection with the Hells Angels, offering some protection from rip-offs and violence.

A person who rips off a Hells Angels-sponsored marijuana grow-op, for example, will have to answer to the Hells Angels and will likely be "taxed"—forced to hand over cash and assets to compensate for the value of the stolen drugs.

Sometimes the Hells Angels take over a formerly independent motorcycle club as a way of expanding into new territory. This is called a "patch over," which involves bikers trading in their former club insignia for the Hells Angels winged Death's Head. That's how the Hells Angels moved into B.C.

Lemieux testified that the Hells Angels started to become a sophisticated organization in 1957 under the leadership of Sonny Ralph Barger of the Oakland chapter. The first chapter expansion outside California took place in New Zealand in 1961. In Canada, the Hells Angels took over the Popeyes gang in Montreal in 1977, followed by a Laval chapter in 1979. In B.C., two chapters of Satan's Angels became Hells Angels in 1983—East End and Nanaimo.

Police say the impetus for the "patch over" of B.C. Satan's Angels was provided by the Hells Angels in Montreal, who have close ties to the Mafia. The Mafia approved of the Hells Angels' expansion to the West Coast to help offload drug shipments by "mother ships" arriving from Asia and Colombia and to transport the drugs to Quebec. This proved to be a profitable alliance that continues to this day, according to police.

Today, the Hells Angels B.C. chapters include the East End, Nanaimo, White Rock, Haney, Mission and Vancouver chapters, the latter having its clubhouse in the Vancouver suburb of Coquitlam.

"Loyalty is the fundamental principle of the Hells Angels . . . This principle is so important that acts of betrayal are punishable by severe sanctions ranging from a beating to [even] death," Lemieux's report said. "Each chapter is self-sufficient in the sense that all of its members have a say in the chapter's decisions, internal disciplinary measures against members and criminal activities of the chapter with regard to its territory [extortion, drug trafficking, etc.]."

Under Hells Angels rules, each chapter has a power structure, making the president absolute leader with veto power over decisions made by members. The vice-president deputizes for the president in his absence.

The sergeant at arms is responsible for discipline at club meetings, funerals and special events. The secretary-treasurer keeps minutes of club meetings and manages the club's finances, including collecting member dues and fines and paying club bills and expenses. He also sometimes acts as an intelligence officer, gathering information about police and rivals, according to police.

The road captain is in charge of organizing mandatory club runs, determining the ultimate destination and any stops for food and gas. If questions arise about anything involving criminal activity at club meetings, "they are presented on a chalk board that is later erased or on paper that is later burned or otherwise destroyed," according to Lemieux.

"The Hells Angels collect intelligence on rival biker gangs and the police," Lemieux said. "The Hells Angels also use women to acquire intelligence regarding rivals and police officers. The women are placed in key positions, for example, with the military, as air traffic controllers and with different government agencies to provide valuable information and service for the bikers." A woman clerk working in the motor vehicle branch, for example, can run a licence plate for a Hells Angel to supply an address to match a phone number, even unlisted numbers.

Lemieux says Hells Angels members work in cells—small groups of trusted people, including criminal associates. Often, the lower level people will not know who the head man is, minimizing the chance of a full-patch member being arrested. Occasionally, however, police arrest top-echelon associates such as Norman Rosenblum of Vancouver who was arrested in 1995 after an RCMP undercover operation that began in Colombia and ended in Montreal.

Rosenblum told an undercover operator that he was a drug importation coordinator—court documents say he reported directly to Montreal drug trafficker Luis Cantieri, whom the *Montreal Gazette* once described as "one of the kingpins of a drug network with connections to Mafia bosses Vito Rizzuto and Frank Cotroni."

Rosenblum was aboard a boat off the coast of Colombia when 558 kilograms of cocaine were transferred to an undercover police vessel. The drugs were destined for Hells Angels International in London, England. Rosenblum, who was arrested with 40 others, was sentenced to 13 years in prison for his role in the drug and money-laundering scheme. Meanwhile, his next-door neighbors in a wealthy part of Vancouver thought he was just a rich businessman who often traveled.

• • •

Port Moody police inspector Andy Richards, who spent 17 years with the Vancouver police anti-biker squad and the Organized Crime Agency of B.C., admits that many of the old-time Hells Angels joined because they love motorcycles and for the camaraderie the club offers. It is a brotherhood that gives members a sense of power and belonging, and offers strength in numbers when it comes to fights.

Today, however, most of the younger guys are in it for the power and the respect that the Hells Angels patch commands, he says. "The younger guys see it as a real entrepreneurial activity to get into the club, to have that protective layer around you, to make money," Richards explained.

The Hells Angels in B.C. have so far avoided the kind of bloody turf war that erupted on Montreal streets with the rival Rock Machine gang in the 1990s, resulting in more than 100 people killed, including an innocent 11-year-old boy. The boy's death caused public outrage and sparked the political will and funding to target the biker gangs and prosecute them on charges of murder, extortion, drug trafficking and living off the profits of prostitution.

In B.C., police say the Hells Angels have operated largely unopposed by rival biker gangs, allowing them to consolidate operations and expand outside of the urban centers into the far reaches of B.C., especially in the oil patch in the north of the province and the oil sands in Alberta, where there is plenty of fast cash to spend on drugs.

As a result, police say, the last decade has seen a rise in street drug activity and its spinoff effects, including rising insurance rates to cover residential and business break-ins undertaken to support drug habits and the damage caused to homes by B.C.'s booming marijuana-growing operations, which are estimated to bring in up to $7 billion a year, tax-free.

High-potency marijuana, known as B.C. Bud, is the province's number one cash crop. Grow-ops are run by every criminal group—Asian gangs, Mafia, the Hells Angels—because the operations produce large amounts of cash that can be used to fund other criminal activity, expand operations and buy legitimate businesses that can be used to launder drug profits. (The term "laundering money" came from the time of 1920s gangster Al Capone, who bought laundromats with his Prohibition-era sales of liquor.)

B.C. Bud is not only distributed in B.C., but across Canada and into the United States, using smuggling methods limited only by the imagination of the criminal mind: logging trucks carrying hollowed out logs; trucks with false bottoms and secret compartments; low-flying helicopters that make quick drops across the border and are able to depart in seconds; and human couriers with backpacks hiking through the woods in remote areas.

In the United States, B.C. marijuana is traded pound for pound for cocaine, which is then smuggled back into Canada. Guns are also smuggled into Canada from the United States because of more lax gun registration laws south of the border. According to the National Weapons Enforcement Support Team, a Canadian agency formed in 2001 to respond to gun smuggling and the trafficking of illegal weapons, 94 percent of crime guns—that is, guns used in crimes ranging from drive-by shootings to murders—seized on Vancouver streets come from the United States, with 64 percent originating from Washington State, followed by California, Oregon, Alaska and Texas.

Guns have now become the weapon of choice in the drug trade, largely to protect the huge amounts of cash that are part of the trade. Profits have been used by Hells Angels to establish legitimate businesses such as nightclubs, trucking firms, travel agencies, coffee bars and hip-hop clothing stores.

The public generally won't know that a business is owned by a Hells Angels member, since many Hells Angels use nominees—trusted associates who register companies in their names in order to hide assets. In recent years, Hells Angels have also registered expensive real estate in the names of spouses or friends, in case the government tries to seize the property as the proceeds of crime.

CHAPTER 4
The Business of Murder

For years, the RCMP has identified outlaw motorcycle gangs in B.C.—the Hells Angels and its puppet clubs—as its prime targets in organized criminal investigations. But for years, the Hells Angels have prospered and expanded while remaining under the radar of the public, if not the police. There had not been a significant prosecution of a Hells Angels member in B.C. until 2001, when two East End chapter members, Chico Pires and Ronaldo Lising, were convicted of cocaine trafficking and sent to prison for four and a half years.

The general public is not normally affected by Hells Angels' activities or violence, unless they are being supplied with drugs to feed a habit or racking up debts with the Angels. While by all accounts Angels make good neighbors because of the lower break-in rates in their immediate vicinity, this is largely due to the fact that they have perfected their methods of instilling fear of retaliation in witnesses. And there has been a mounting list of murders believed to be connected to the Angels, many remaining unsolved.

Most of the Hells Angels' violence is directed at "grow rips"—rip-off marijuana grow operations that compete with the Hells Angels in their territory—and the failure of drug dealers to pay drug debts. Of course, Hells Angels don't turn to the police for help when someone rips them off. They take care of it themselves, and sometimes people end up dead, which is one of the reasons the Hells Angels have such a fearsome reputation in the criminal underworld.

Hells Angels members rarely do their own dirty work, which is why very few end up in jail, police say. Instead, they contract jobs out to associates or trusted hitmen. Contract killer Mickie (Phil) Smith confessed to a mob boss—actually an undercover police officer—that one of his victims was 33-year-old Paul Percy Soluk, who had ripped off a Hells Angels marijuana grow-op.

In a video played at Smith's Vancouver trial, the killer explained he was told by an Asian gangster named Brian, who arranged the murder, that the Soluk hit was undertaken on behalf of the East End chapter of the Hells Angels.

Police never found the body of Soluk, who was killed in 1999. Smith, a 56-year-old former life insurance salesman convicted of five murders, confessed to the undercover officer that Soluk was located in a Surrey crack house and taken to a nearby garage, where he was shot.

A boat was supposed to pick up the body and dump it at sea, but it never appeared. Instead, Smith said a man called Yurik helped chop up the body and dispose of the remains at the local garbage dump. "He's not an Angel but he works with the Angels," Smith said of Yurik. "I know he's done lots of hits." The Smith case underscores how Hells Angels distance themselves from crimes that could otherwise put them behind bars for life.

The list of murders police believe have links to the Hells Angels in B.C. grows each year, and sometimes involves complex homicide investigations that lead detectives out of the country.

That was the case with the 1990 murder of former Vancouver stockbroker John (Ray) Ginnetti, who was killed in his West Vancouver home. Ginnetti had at one time been a partner in a lucrative lottery-ticket resale business, but had sold the business and was planning to move to Las Vegas. He had previously made a good living as a stockbroker, helping Hells Angels members to capitalize on their investments, and Hells Angels members attended Ginnetti's funeral to pay their respects.

Five years after the murder, police eventually tracked down Ginnetti's killer, a Cuban national, Jose Raul Perez-Valdez, who by then was serving time in the United States for kidnapping and possession of cocaine. After finishing his eight-year sentence, he was extradited to Vancouver on Christmas Eve 2003. Two years later, the hitman pleaded guilty to the $30,000 contract killing, which was arranged by former Hells Angels enforcer Roger Daggitt, who had had a falling-out with Ginnetti. A plea bargain included the hitman cooperating with police in exchange for being given a new identity.

Less than a week after Ginnetti was killed—the day of Ginnetti's funeral in fact—Russian-born gangster Sergey Filonov was gunned down outside Trev Deeley Motorcycles, then located on East Broadway. Miroslav Michal and Shannon Aldrich were charged with Filonov's murder but the charges were later stayed when Filonov's brother, Taras, who witnessed his brother's fatal shooting and was struck with a hammer before he fled the scene, refused to cooperate with police.

There was bad blood between the Hells Angels and Filonov and his Russian-born gangster buddies, who had brazenly ripped off the Hells Angels during a $250,000 cocaine deal. The Russians had arranged to buy some coke but left without paying after drawing guns and grabbing the drugs. Taras Filonov, Sergey's brother, was subsequently kidnapped and held for a $200,000 ransom. Taras was released after the ransom was paid, but the kidnappers vowed the Russians would pay in blood.

Two years after his brother's fatal shooting, Taras Filonov was found dead in a forested area of the University of British Columbia, his hands cuffed behind his back, his face blown off by a shotgun. Police could identify him only through fingerprints.

Another member of the Russian gang, Eugeniy Alekseev, had two of his cars blown up in Vancouver but was not seriously injured by either blast. One of the bombings occurred after he and his brother Alexander had reportedly just finished dinner with Pavel Bure, a Russian-born hockey player then with the Vancouver Canucks. When Eugeniy started his own car using his remote starter, it detonated the bomb, but he escaped unhurt.

Alexander Alekseev disappeared and is presumed dead. In 1995, Eugeniy Alekseev, then 26, was found dead in a luxury hotel room in Mexico City with what was believed to be a self-inflicted gunshot wound to the head. "Maybe there was no place left to run," a Vancouver investigator said at the time. Police didn't feel foul play was involved or that the Angels had tracked him to Mexico.

Former Hells Angels enforcer Roger Daggitt was shot three times in the head at the age of 39 while having a beer with his son at the Turf Hotel in Surrey on October 6, 1992. Daggitt had arranged Ginnetti's $30,000 contract killing and, according to a Los Angeles informant, was the getaway driver for the hitman who killed Ginnetti.

Montreal contract killer Serge Robin pleaded guilty to Daggitt's murder—Robin was suspected of killing three people after flying into Vancouver. He was already serving a life sentence and was on parole for a 1977 Quebec murder when he walked away from a halfway house. He pleaded guilty to killing Daggitt after learning he had a contract on his life—his plea was made in exchange for being moved out of B.C. to serve his time. The sudden plea came mid-trial after the names of Montreal Mafia boss Frank Cotroni and other Quebec mobsters were raised in court by Robin's lawyer during the cross-examination of a Crown witness, who was in police protection. At Robin's trial, a judge denied the defense lawyer's request to obtain documents seized from a raid on a Hells Angels clubhouse in Quebec.

The following year, on April 30, 1993, Michael (Zeke) Mickle, the president of the Nanaimo chapter of the Hells Angels, disappeared and is presumed dead. He reportedly owed his fellow Hells Angels a large amount of money related to a cocaine shipment that went awry. Police also investigated a tip that he was killed by Vietnamese drug dealers on Vancouver Island, who wanted to show they weren't afraid of the Hells Angels. The case remains open.

Four years later, on June 2, 1997, Ernie Ozolins, 41, and his girlfriend Lisa Chamberlain, 32, were shot execution-style at Ozolins' West Vancouver home. Ozolins had left the Haney chapter of the Hells Angels after he developed a drug problem and reportedly misappropriated funds. About 100 Hells Angels on Harleys attended his West Vancouver funeral. The case remains unsolved.

Hells Angels associate Manuel (Manny) Valenti was fatally shot in front of his wife and child on October 5, 2000. Valenti had completed a 50-kilogram cocaine deal with Hells Angels member Donald William (Donny) Roming, before Roming was shot to death. Valenti had connections to the Commisso crime family in Toronto. Police believe Valenti was involved in a conflict with bikers over a guy who ran a marijuana grow operation sponsored by a Haney Hells Angels member. The murder was a contract killing.

Roming was fatally shot outside the Bar None nightclub in downtown Vancouver on March 8, 2001, after an argument inside the club with a group of men linked to John Rogers. The next month, on April 29, Rogers was shot to death outside a Vancouver gas station. He knew he was a target and was wearing a bulletproof vest at the time of the shooting. Shortly beforehand, Hells Angels associate Rick Alexander was arrested by police outside the residence of a prime suspect in the Roming murder. In Alexander's car the cops found two handguns and an alleged "hit list" that included the names of Rogers and his buddies who were outside Bar None when Roming was killed. Alexander was convicted on weapons charges, but Rogers' execution remains unsolved.

The next year, Haney chapter Hells Angels member Rick (Blackie) Burgess was reported missing on January 7. He reportedly had drug and money problems. He was declared legally dead in 2004, but his disappearance has never been solved.

On August 16, 2003, in the worst nightclub incident in Vancouver history, 10 people were shot and three were killed by gunfire at the Loft Six nightclub in the Gastown area of Vancouver when a gunfight broke out between two rival groups of gang members. Among the innocent bystanders killed was John Popovich, 32, of Windsor, Ontario, who had worked as a local deejay and was celebrating his planned return to Windsor with friends. Another innocent bystander was Los Angeles hip-hop dance instructor Steve Stanton, 30, who was shot in the back while with friends. He returned to L.A. confined to a wheelchair.

Among the 200 people in Loft Six when gunfire erupted was Nomads Hells Angels member Jamie Holland. Asian and East Indian gangsters were also in the nightclub. Police believe the dispute arose after someone recognized John Johnson, 31, one of those fatally shot. He had worked as a bouncer at Brandi's strip lounge, where he had beaten an East Indian gangster to a pulp. Johnson later learned the man was a gangster and went into hiding.

Before the club became Loft Six, it was owned by Hells Angels member Donald Roming. The club has since reopened as the Diamond restaurant.

• • •

With this litany of violence in mind, Plante had plenty of reasons to be nervous about infiltrating the Hells Angels. Plante took some comfort in the fact that, as the E-Pandora investigation began to shift into Phase II, many of his interactions with Hells Angels were secretly recorded by a police cover team. Police installed a tiny video recorder in the trunk of Plante's car, so they could videotape what he was loading into the vehicle and have visuals of the people he was dealing with.

Plante also wore a listening device—known as a wire. Where it was placed on his body is a closely guarded secret of an undercover police unit known as Special I, which also installs tiny listening devices, commonly known as "bugs," covertly in the homes and vehicles of targets of criminal investigations.

In a conversation secretly recorded by Plante in May 2004, John Punko discussed how police had unexpectedly shown up twice at planned meetings with a man named Parminder Gill. Punko and Lising were trying to collect a large sum of money from Gill for Punko's childhood friend, Leroy Pereira. The collection started off well, then became a problem.

Parminder Gill had arranged to meet to make payments, but at the same time anonymous calls were made to 911, causing police to show up where the payments were supposed to be made. In responding to the 911 calls, police were able to identify Pereira and Punko as the men who were at the places where the anonymous caller reported there would be two troublesome criminals.

On May 26, 2004, Plante's device caught Punko counseling Plante to put a scare into Gill to keep him from talking to police. The meeting took place at Punko's home. The biker sounded worried, explaining he believed Gill had gone to the police. "If he phoned the cops, it's pretty bad," Punko said. "I think we're fucking busted."

"Think we're bein' followed or what?" Plante asked, with the television on in the background. The worried tone of the conversation was oddly punctuated by a TV sitcom's laugh track several times.

"I don't know. I, I don't think so, but Ronnie [Lising] thinks they might be fuckin' gatherin' up warrants for us three right now. Know what I mean?"

Punko said he wasn't sure yet. "It's like a fifty-fifty right now, I'll tell you what's goin' on. Anyways, uh, I talked to Ronnie an' George, an' we met him, we met him a few times, eh. Supposed to have the money a couple of days ago. Well, he's delayin', delayin'. Now he's supposed to have it today, delayin'. Now he says 'Friday for sure, no doubt about it.' But we met him for a second time today, an' fuckin' cops were everywhere. Like five cop cars fuckin' swarmed in on us. Anyways, then they're askin', what's uh, 'cause they did this a second time, before, a week ago."

"Maybe somebody's playin' a joke or somethin' like that," Plante suggested. "Anyways, we put two an' two together. It's Parm, right. Fuckin'. Just to get off, get us off his ass."

"You never know," Punko continued. "Or, or he's gonna pay us this Friday. The fuckin' piece of shit. He's finished. Anyways, um, I'm gonna get a hold of, Brian's gonna come here, and uh, he wants you to fuckin' uh . . . he wants you to go over right now, an' see where his parents live, and if you two go, he wants you to go fuckin' rip, rip that fuckin' place apart."

"No problem, man. Fuck. No fuckin' problem," Plante said.

"Be very careful when you do it, right," Punko advised. "Gotta show that we're not fuckin' afraid of the cops. 'Cause that'll back him right down by pressing charges, an' . . . You know what I mean?"

"Yeah," Plante responded. "Oh, fuck. What a fuckin' nightmare."

"Fuckin' piece of shit," Punko said.

"Like a fuckin' Molotov cock-, ju-, anything just to fuckin' scare him. We don't wanna hurt anybody," Punko told Plante. "I think he just phoned the cops, just to buy time."

Plante agreed. "That's what I think, too."

"But you know . . . he went over the edge, he phoned the cops now," Punko said. "Parm has told them everything."

"Well, what would they arrest you for?" Plante asked.

"There's been money already exchanged. Three hundred grand, right?" Punko explained.

"Extortion," Plante said.

"Extortion, yeah," Punko responded. "Threatening. It doesn't matter."

Another man, Brian Jung, was later heard joining the conversation. Punko told Jung what had happened.

"Are we even gonna try to find out where he lives, he's living right now? 'Cause he's not living at home," Jung said.

"At his parents' house," Punko pointed out, bringing Jung up to speed.

"I know where his parents live. He's not living at home," Jung offered.

"Fuck. Do you know where his parents live?" Punko asked, his spirits perking up.

"Yeah. I went and knocked up on the door one day," Jung replied.

"Where do they, where do they live?" Punko asked.

"Out in Surrey, South Surrey, huge fuckin' property. Shitty house, but huge property," Jung said.

"I'll get Leroy to take him out there," Punko said. " 'Cause when we get, hey, this, if we go down, he's gonna go there and fuckin' rip, rip it apart. He's a fuckin' goof, man."

Punko turned to Plante. "Hey, so you don't mind goin' out there?"

"No problem," Plante said.

"Fuck sakes. Thanks, buddy." Punko sounded relieved.

"So we're goin' to see uh, Leroy right now, right?" Plante asked.

"Yeah," Punko said. "You can drive out with him, probably drive out with Brian to see where it is. Just so you know."

"Yeah," Plante agreed.

"Fuckin' go by and light it up," Punko urged Plante, who understood this to mean to do a drive-by shooting at Gill's parents' house to send Gill an ominous message.

"I'll do it for sure, fuck, I'll do it," Plante said.

"Yeah if you do it, that's fuckin' cool, man," Punko said.

"I got no problems doing it," Plante told him. "Yeah, you ask me to do it, I'll do it, bro."

"But anyways, that's it," Punko said. "I hope everything's okay Friday. So hey, go do that quickly. Go to his parents' house, and just find out exactly where he lives. 'Cause you know why? 'Cause if it goes down, we're gonna rip it up, an' just make a message that cops don't fuckin' scare us. Okay?"

"You know who knows where he probably lives is fuckin' the other guy. His fuckin' guy," Jung said.

"I don't care about him," Punko said. "I want his parents. His fuckin' parents. . . . Hey, if you go there and his parents have a moving truck there and it looks like they're moving out, we're toast. I'll tell you right now. It's . . . we're fuckin' finished."

In another conversation, Lising was overheard by police talking about an encounter he had with Parminder Gill around the same time. He said Gill "got mouthy on the phone" and made threats against his mom and dad, so Lising went and "pounded" him.

"If there wasn't so much money involved he would have been fuckin' . . . I told him, you're lucky . . . we keep you alive . . . I know that you are gonna pay," Lising said.

Before going to the home, Plante, Punko and Jung met with Leroy Pereira at the Stones Throw pub in Burnaby. Pereira, who owned a hydroponics store, drove out with Plante to Gill's parents' home, but the police agent did not "rip up" the home or "light it up."

Pereira would later be charged, along with Punko and Jung, with the extortion of Gill. The Crown later stayed the charge against Jung. Pereira pleaded guilty and was sentenced to two years, but a jury eventually acquitted Punko of extortion. The jury, however, did convict Punko of counseling Plante to commit mischief (damaging property in a drive-by shooting) even though Plante never carried out Punko's request.

· · ·

In July 2004, Plante was asked by Lising to join him on a drive with Punko to Kelowna, where Plante was supposed to "keep an eye out for cops" while they were in town to collect money from a man who can only be identified as "C.P."—the man was later granted a publication ban of his name by a B.C. Supreme Court judge.

C.P. grew marijuana and acted as a "broker," charging a fee for smuggling B.C. Bud to the United States. One 140-kilogram load had been lost and C.P.'s "clients" thought he had ripped them off. The clients went to Lising and another full-patch Hells Angels member, asking them to collect the payment due from C.P. for the "ripped off" load. Lising demanded $50,000 from C.P.

During the five-hour drive to Kelowna, Lising shared his thoughts with Plante about membership in the Hells Angels, saying it was an opportunity to make money and how violence was necessary to maintain club supremacy.

Plante's wire also picked up Lising discussing his respect for a certain Hells Angels member, partly because of the biker's willingness to fight rival biker clubs such as the Bandidos.

"He rode his bike all the time, everywhere. I liked that about him. He was a total club guy, he told me a lot of stories about the club. He was a—well, he was a good member, man. He wanted to go to fuckin', to fuckin' Europe to fight them, fuckin' punch out Bandidos, man," Lising said.

Later on during the drive, Lising discussed his life as a Hells Angel, which allowed him the opportunity to make money: "No, but listen man, ya know I've been in the club for fuckin' seven years now. Fuck, it took a long time to make fuckin', I was broke for a long time. I was broke. The day I got my patch, my fuckin' jewelry was in the pawn shop for sale, in a store for sale, man, broke."

Lising explained that some members don't get what being a Hells Angel is all about. "It took me a long time to make money, and here he is with an opportunity of a lifetime. . . . I mean, you're gonna have a fuckin' few bucks in your pocket and be a Hells Angel? Fuck man. You know, that's like the top of my world," the biker explained about another Hells Angels member who didn't take the opportunity seriously.

"You know and he's like, takin' off, fuckin' and you got fuckin' money to be made, you know, and not callin' me. Losin' his phone and not gettin' another one, you know like we're doin' somethin' here. You know, it's all a risk man, there's a risk in, it's, ya know, you gotta fuckin' weigh out the fuckin' risk and fuck, ya know, and rewards, right, ya know what I mean?" Lising continued.

"Is it worth it, the risk for this reward, right? Obviously to him it's not. With me, that's what I do. Is this gonna be worth me getting hit and goin' away, ya know, away from my children, my kids? I got kids to support. Ya know, obviously it is 'cause ya know, that's what I want. So you know, I put my ass on the line. I thought, you know fine, he's not a talker guy, I do the talkin', I'll handle everything. I told him an' George too. George was like . . . I need to fuckin' do this? Fuck, don't make me do that too, man, then I'm doin' it all. How do I fuckin' feel about that? Well here you go, here's half a mil for you. I did everything, I did the talkin', I did spending, I did the fuckin', then I did the job. Ya know?"

Lising also told Plante his views about dealing with the upstart UN gang.

"That's what you tell these fuckin', fucking UN cocks, they're just fucking faggots," the biker said. "First of all, those guys are not fucking welcome. They're not welcome in this fuckin' province. They ain't fucking allowed. If you see 'em, we're gonna fuckin' take care of 'em, and anybody who does anything with 'em, talks to 'em, does this with 'em, hangs out with 'em, is gonna be treated the same fuckin' way. Hells Angel or not. See who fuckin' stands up. They do, we pound 'em. That's what Oakland used to do, eh? Oakland would hold a fuckin' meeting, full charter. Tell 'em how it is. Any member caught fuckin' talkin' to a guy that they kicked out of the club, fuckin' will get treated like him, too. That's the way it should be man."

Police also listened to another conversation as Punko shared his views with Plante about the UN gang, saying the Hells Angels should be the only gang in town. "Yeah, but ya know what, this is Hells Angels. There should be no other fuckin' gangs poppin' up around, ya know what I mean?" Punko said. "And what the fuck are you doing bringing a gang in our fuckin' town, man."

After arriving in Kelowna, police watched as Punko and Lising met with C.P., who was carrying a lunch bucket. Police also watched Lising and C.P. walk inside a Canadian Tire store.

Later, Lising had another meeting with C.P. at a Kelowna-area car wash, then still another attended by Lising, Punko and Vancouver chapter Hells Angels member Guy Rossignol, who owned a house in Kelowna.

Two months later, Lising asked Plante to go to Kelowna and pick up a phone from C.P. The biker instructed Plante to go to a car lot owned by Dave Revell, a Hells Angels associate, who would arrange the meeting with C.P. The next morning, Plante went to a car wash and met C.P., who handed over the phone, which Plante gave to Lising later that day when they met at a Greek restaurant on Canada Way in Burnaby.

Lising then asked Plante to tend the bar that night at the East End clubhouse, which Plante did. He didn't get home until 5 a.m.

At a later meeting at the clubhouse with Hells Angels members David Giles, Bruce Skreptak and Damiano Dipopolo, Giles asked Plante if he had been instructed to go to Kelowna and "deliver a message." Plante nodded. Giles advised that wasn't a good idea right now because Lising had "a lot of heat on him." Giles also asked if "Brother Love" knew about it. Plante knew that was a reference to Hells Angels member Louie Robinson.

Little did the Angels know that Plante was working for the police, who wanted their agent to keep meeting with Lising to get more details about the extortion of C.P. On September 8, Plante went to Lising's home, where the biker instructed Plante to drive to Hope to pick up $10,000 cash from C.P.

"As soon as you get there, if there are any questions, text me," Lising said.

Plante drove to Hope, located about 200 kilometers east of Vancouver, and sat in a restaurant, where C.P. gave the undercover agent $5,000 cash wrapped in a newspaper. During their 20-minute meeting, C.P. received a text message from Lising that said: "Hey fuck face, that's not what you promised."

It took C.P. some time to get Lising off his back—the drug dealer had initially phoned Hells Angels member Guy Rossignol, known as Bully, to act as his advocate, trying to get the Hells Angels to realize the drug seizure wasn't his fault. He explained to Bully that the pot had been seized by police.

C.P. eventually got his lawyer in Alberta to call the RCMP about the missing load. The lawyer then wrote a letter explaining that the pot, contained in nine hockey bags, had been seized by the RCMP in Alberta and police in Montana during a cross-border smuggling bust.

C.P. got a friend to give the letter to Hells Angels member Richard Goldammer, asking him to show his fellow bikers that it wasn't his fault the pot had been seized. After Rossignol got involved in the dispute, Lising accused Rossignol of protecting a rip-off. Lising told Plante that C.P. was getting cocky because he was being protected by Rossignol. Eventually, however, Lising had a change of heart.

C.P. eventually received a text message from Lising saying, "Good luck. We don't want your money." By that time, C.P. had paid about $25,000 to satisfy Lising's demands.

• • •

On October 3, 2004, Randy Potts phoned his mother, Donna, to proudly advise that he had become a full-patch member of the Hells Angels. Police also listened while the biker told his brother about the potential rewards of obtaining his patch. Potts complained at one point that he had had to "look after 21 grown men for two and a half years" while in the recruitment program.

The night Potts got his patch, Giles sent Plante to go buy some cigars. Plante also tended bar and cooked food for the party to celebrate Potts becoming a full-patch member.

Days later, on October 11, 2004, Potts ordered Plante to pick up a cache of guns at the Surrey home of Potts' mother. The biker was worried that police had raided the home of his estranged wife, seizing four barrels of dimethyl sulfone, a precursor chemical needed to cook methamphetamine. Potts told Plante to get a hockey bag and pick up the guns, which were hidden at the mobile home of his mother and stepfather.

"Go over there right now and, and put all the stuff in the bag," Potts said.

"A big gym bag?" Plante asked.

"A goalie bag," Potts replied.

Plante went to a Sportmart store in Langley to purchase a hockey bag, then drove to Potts' parents' home, where Potts' stepfather, Jack, led Plante to a cubicle storage area at the back of his trailer.* Plante pulled out a box and several bags, which he placed in the hockey bag and turned over to police that evening. Inside were four grenades, four silencers and six firearms—a .45-caliber Colt semiautomatic pistol, an Intratec 9-mm semiautomatic pistol, a Ruger .22-caliber semiautomatic rifle, a Franchi .22-caliber semiautomatic rifle, a Voere bolt-action rifle and a Ruger .44 Magnum revolver. Plante was told by Potts to hold the guns for safekeeping.

Two weeks later, Plante arranged to buy 26 ounces of cocaine from Potts for $28,000. Inspector Shinkaruk put the cash in a yellow Sportmart bag, which Plante gave to Potts outside the Green Timbers Pub. As arranged with Potts, Plante then went to meet Potts' buddy, Chad Barroby, at a Coffee King shop, where Barroby handed over a knapsack containing the cocaine.

Plante felt he was on a roll. He was selling meth to the bikers and buying cocaine from them. The police hoped he would move up the "food chain" and start buying from more senior Hells Angels. His next target was close to the heart of the East End chapter's president, John Bryce—his son Jonathan.

Like Plante, Bryce's son was an "official friend" of the East End Hells Angels, the bottom rung of the recruitment program. He had agreed to sell Plante a kilogram of cocaine for $20,000. On November 13, 2004, Bryce Jr. brought the cocaine to an ABC Country Restaurant, where they exchanged the cash and drugs from the trunk of Plante's car, with the hidden camera recording the transaction.

Two days later, Jonathan Bryce sold Plante another kilogram of cocaine for $24,000. Bryce brought the kilo to the East End clubhouse where Plante was working. There was an unwritten rule, Plante would later recall, that Hells Angels were never supposed

---

* The parents were not charged.

to do drug deals at the clubhouse, because they could attract "heat" from police.

Plante told Jonathan Bryce that he would go get the money, which his RCMP handlers gave him. But when Plante returned to the clubhouse, Bryce Jr. was playing hockey, so the police agent had to cool his heels waiting for Bryce to get back.

Plante would later make a final purchase of two kilos of cocaine from Bryce Jr., which also took place at the East End Hells Angels clubhouse. Plante was indeed making his way up the ladder.

CHAPTER 5

Our Missing Friend

Michael Plante was badly beaten on October 15, 2004, during a fight outside Brandi's Exotic Nightclub by a member of the rival United Nations gang, not once, but twice. After his first thumping, Plante returned, looking for a rematch, which again ended badly for him.

The incident began as a confrontation between Hells Angels member Ronnie Lising and members of the UN gang. Plante interceded and got into a fight with a huge, heavily tattooed UN gang member believed to be John William Croitoru, a former professional wrestler known as "K-9" who is now facing charges of conspiracy to commit murder of the notorious Bacon brothers, as well as the first-degree murder of Jonathan Barber, an innocent man who was mistaken for one of the Bacon brothers. Plante was knocked out cold on the pavement by his opponent, who was a close buddy of then-UN gang leader Clay Roueche, now serving 30 years for drug trafficking in a U.S. prison.

Brandi's was a well-known upscale strip club located on the fifth floor of an office building at Dunsmuir and Hornby, in the heart of Vancouver's financial district. At the time, it was a known hangout for Hells Angels members and, in 2003, became notorious for another reason—Hollywood actor Ben Affleck got into hot water after it became public that he was reportedly entertained at the club by lap-dancer Tammy Morris and other dancers. Affleck, who had gone there with his actor buddy Christian Slater, Slater's wife, Ryan Haddon, and actress Tara Reid, maintained that nothing out of the ordinary had happened. But after the dancer sold her story for a reported $100,000 to the *National Enquirer*, Jennifer Lopez broke off her engagement to Affleck, who threatened legal action against the tabloid.

Brandi's liquor licence was temporarily suspended in 2007 after police expressed concerns that there was a risk of serious violence at the club because it was frequented by members of the Hells Angels and the UN gang.

The UN gang, which at the time was heavily involved in exporting high-potency B.C. Bud to the United States in exchange for cocaine and guns, derives its name from the fact its three dozen core members are from diverse ethnic backgrounds—Caucasian, Iranian, Asian and East Indian Canadians.

A police report alleged that a prominent local Vancouver Hells Angels Nomads member, Gino Zumpano, was directly involved in the management of Brandi's. Zumpano was considered one of the wealthiest Hells Angels at the time, living in a home worth well over $1 million. It publicly emerged that he had owned various legitimate businesses in town; for example, his investment company, GPAV Investments, had in 2004 held a total of 2.6 million shares—then worth more than $5 million—in House of

Brussels Chocolates, which had a manufacturing plant and retail outlets in Vancouver.

Zumpano was also involved in another company, G.J.P Holdings, that bought the Spinning Wheel nightclub in Gastown in 2003 for $800,000. The premises, later sold for a tidy profit, is now home to the popular Irish Heather pub. One of the directors of that Zumpano company was a Nomads member named Jamie Holland, who was once convicted of carrying a loaded handgun with its serial number removed. Holland was among the 200 patrons in the nearby Loft Six club, where 10 people were shot, three fatally, during a shootout between rival gangsters in August 2003—the worst nightclub shooting in Vancouver.

"Our specific concern with Brandi's is that members of the Hells Angels and the United Nations gangs are often in attendance and police intelligence indicates a serious rift has occurred between these two crime groups which will likely result in serious violence," said a report by Vancouver police inspector Adua Porteous.

The report revealed that officers had been called to Brandi's more than 70 times in 2006, resulting in 29 police reports, including 15 that were directly related to the presence of identified gang members in the club.

There were a number of Hells Angels and associates at Brandi's the night Plante was badly beaten. He was angry and upset that none of the bikers stepped in to help him. He was also angry that, although he had phoned his police handlers before the fight, they hadn't shown up either. A wiretap picked up an enraged Plante later making a threatening phone call, presumably to a brother.

"I'm going to come over to your house now and I'm going to shoot your fucking brains out. How about that?" Plante spat out. Plante later admitted he was in a rage but had no plan to carry out his threat. "My face was all beaten up. I had headaches. I was a mess," he said.

When police finally reached him by phone a few days later, Plante yelled at his handler and gave him an earful. "I tried calling them for two days and they wouldn't answer," Plante would later recall. "I was ready to quit." Pissed off, he told his police handlers he was done—he couldn't take the pressure any more. They convinced him to hang in a little longer.

During the discussion, Plante said he was tired of dealing with Potts and Punko, whom he referred to as "mopes" and "goofuses."

"We got to get around these two mopes and get onto something else here," Plante told his handlers.

He wanted to go after the members of the local Hells Angels Nomads because, after five East End chapter members left to go with the Nomads, what remained was a "geriatric crew . . . a bunch of old farts," Plante complained, referring to the fact that many of the East End members were in their fifties.

"I was concerned, I mean, in the East End there wasn't many guys left that were, you know, going to allow me to make illegal money with them," Plante later recalled of that discussion with police.

Bob Paulson, then an RCMP inspector who was "running the show," as Plante described the E-Pandora investigation, agreed that police wanted to move up the Hells Angels food chain and nail senior members believed to be involved in drug trafficking. But he wasn't convinced Plante had established enough trust with the Nomads.

• • •

After the Brandi's beating, Stanley Gillis, then-sergeant at arms of the East End chapter, asked Plante to provide details of the assault. He told Plante to find out who in the UN gang had assaulted him and promised that he (Gillis) would help take care of the guy.

During a meeting of the East End chapter on December 2, 2004, Plante was again asked to provide details of the assault, this time by Hells Angels member David Giles. He told Plante after the meeting to find out where the individual and his girlfriend lived, and Giles would deal with them.

Following another meeting of the East End chapter on January 3, 2005, Plante again provided details of the assault. Giles then told Plante and Randy Potts to "get their masks on" and to take care of the guy who had punched out Plante—this conversation was secretly recorded by police. Plante took Giles' comments to mean put on balaclavas and "get rid of the guy" but nothing ever came of it.

Police also heard members of the East End chapter discussing a debt collection from Clay Roueche, then head of the UN gang. Police believed Giles was involved in the collection, which allegedly stemmed from a failed marijuana delivery involving two UN gang associates. Plante told police investigators that Giles had tasked Hells Angels member Joseph Bruce Skreptak with collecting the debt. But no charges were ever laid.

• • •

Plante, meanwhile, continued his dealings with Potts, who took Plante with him for a meeting on November 17, 2004, in the parking lot of the Four Rinks in Langley. Potts believed that one of the marijuana grow operations of his friend Chad Barroby had been ripped off, and suspected that the man they were meeting, Brad MacElhinney, and someone named Melanie Murphy might have been involved.*

---

* MacElhinney and Murphy were not charged.

The conversation was picked up by the wire worn by Plante, who understood his role was to be intimidating.

"So, uh . . . I wanna ask ya about, and uh, I don't want you to lie to me, 'kay?" Potts asked MacElhinney, who agreed. " 'Cause that won't be in your favor," Potts pointed out.

"No, I know, yeah," MacElhinney responded.

"Yeah, so um, a good friend a mine, a year and a half . . . come to me about a partner of his [that] ripped him off, brought up your name. But now, about five people have come forward."

"I don't, I wouldn't lie about somethin' like that," MacElhinney said.

"All we wanna do is to let you know we're gonna get to the bottom of it," Potts said.

"And, and you guys are who you are right? So . . . fuck, I'm gonna lie. That's just fuckin' insane, right? 'Cause it all comes out in the wash, ya know, it really does," MacElhinney acknowledged, going on to explain that he knows not to lie because he was in trouble with "your guys' house" before, and he never wants that to happen again. The meeting was observed by two undercover surveillance officers. After the meeting, Potts told Plante: "He's guilty."

Potts and MacElhinney met again that evening in a Home Depot parking lot. After the meeting, Plante suggested to Potts, "We gotta meet him somewhere where it's not fuckin' so public, eh? Next time."

"Ya think so?" Potts responded.

"Well, just so I can thump him out, right?" Plante said.

"He'll be getting a fuckin' thumpin'," Potts agreed.

On December 14, 2005, Plante and Potts met at a Home Depot with another man, D.B., to see if he could provide information about MacElhinney's possible involvement in the rip-off before trying to collect money from MacElhinney.

"I need you to help me out with a few things," Potts told D.B.

"Yeah, sure. No problem," the other man said.

"I wouldn't want you to lie to me or anything," Potts added.

"No, I definitely wouldn't want to either. Ha," D.B. said.

"Got any idea of what I wanna talk to you about?"

"Um, not really."

"Okay, don't lie to me, I'm, I know he let you know that he did it," Potts put to D.B. "You know that he ripped that place off, two years ago."

"A long, long time," D.B. said.

"Yeah, where did, uh, Brad come up with the um, two hundred and fifty grand that you guys were uh, running around and getting exchange . . . him and Quigley, was about twenty months ago?" Potts asked.

Potts brought out a piece of paper, listing all of MacElhinney's assets, which he read to D.B. Potts then told him that Murphy got two guys to rip off three grow houses.

"Well yeah, I just wanna be straight, that's all I knew really," D.B. explained. "I don't wanna to get in trouble with you guys or anything, or follow his, his bad track of being in trouble now, right."

"He's a rip-off," Plante interjected.

"Yeah, yeah," Potts added, "he's already been, he's been in trouble with, with the club once . . . "

Potts went on to tell D.B., "I'm in no hurry to fuckin' crunch him, right. But, I'd like to know when he's puttin' somethin' together, and when he's got a fuckin' nice bundle together and then go see him and talk to him while the bundle's sitting there.

"And if anything comes up that you've maybe forgotten, tell us . . . before we find out that you're involved in this. Just fuckin' cough it out because if you fuckin' tell us right now, we're not

gonna care about it. You just tell us, tell us what the fuck's goin'
on and then we walk."

· · ·

Police also listened in to a phone call to Potts on January 20, 2005,
from a man called "Big Rob," whose real name was Rob Krayem.
Potts was surprised by the call because the phone line was for the
exclusive use of his main drug distributor, Wissam Ayach. The
call, which Potts considered a breach of his security, came about
because Big Rob and Trevor Lyons, known as Cowboy, were
trying to collect a debt owed by Potts' friend, Darren Hoffman,
who at the time was staying with Potts at the North Burnaby Inn
hotel. Hoffman had just got out of jail and Potts was trying to get
Hoffman into rehab for his drug addiction.*

"Um, remember I have an issue with Hoffman and so does
Trevor?" Krayem asked.

"Yeah," Potts said, sounding annoyed that Big Rob even had
his phone number.

"I'll tell you where Hoffman is right now. He's with me. Right
now," Potts informed him. "Alright? We're trying to get him into
fuckin' treatment, he just got outta jail."

"Alright," Krayem said.

"Alright? You guys fucking back off or I'll fuckin' beat your
fuckin' brains in," Potts warned. "Are you, understand that? You
figure that one out? Alright?"

"I never went near him," Krayem pointed out.

"And, however, you better fuckin' figure out how you got
this fuckin' number, you big fat cocksucker, 'cause I'm gonna
come looking for ya. I'm gonna call you back and you're
gonna come and see me, alright? Give the guy [Hoffman] a

* Rob Krayem and Trevor Lyons were not charged.

fucking break and you tell Cowboy that I wanna fuckin' see the cocksucker. You understand?"

A short time later, Potts spoke with Hoffman. "Oh-ho, buddy. Am I ever fucking mad," Potts said.

"Yeah?" Hoffman responded, wondering what had happened.

"You know who just phoned me up about you?" Potts asked.

"Who?" Hoffman asked.

"That [guy who] wants money from you?" Potts explained. "Must'a heard you were out with me, right? ... That fat fucking Rob phoned me on my, on my fucking stupid line that I got. And uh, so he says, 'Oh, we wondered if you could help me get that money out of fucking Hoffman. He owes Cowboy and, I think, four grand or something.'"

"Mm-hmm," Hoffman responded.

"And uh [chuckles] I said, you, fuck you," Potts explained. "What do you want me to do? Get blood from a fucking stone, you fat cunt?" Potts told Hoffman he could forget about the debt, it was taken care of.

In the meantime, Punko had agreed to sell Plante five kilos of cocaine for $112,000, which Plante got from his handlers in a knapsack. He took the money to Punko's house on November 19, 2004.

A week later, Plante was sent to Sherbrooke, Quebec, to help two East End chapter members take part in the 20th anniversary party for the Quebec chapter. Bryce Jr. also went, along with East End Hells Angels members David Giles and Michael Christiansen, whose nickname was Speedy. Christiansen had been a member of the Halifax chapter before he joined the East End Hells Angels, and Giles had been a member of the Sherbrooke chapter. It was also the 20th anniversaries of Giles and Christiansen becoming Hells Angels members.

Once Plante returned from Quebec, he was asked to attend a meeting by Hells Angels member Jean Violette. Also at the meeting was another East End chapter "official friend," Jonathan Bryce Jr. Violette explained they were going meet with an alleged North Vancouver drug dealer, Glen Louie.* At one time, Louie and Bryce Jr. had been roommates. Bryce had given Louie a belt buckle with the Hells Angels insignia on it and Louie had mistakenly thought this gesture of friendship gave him the right to tell people he was connected to the Hells Angels while he was dealing drugs.

"You know who the fuck I am? I'm with the chapter," Louie said during one drug deal, showing off his Hells Angels belt. Louie added he would get five guys over there to "fuck him up."

This got back to Violette, who discussed it with several senior East End Hells Angels. They decided that Louie was using the club's name without permission so needed to be taught a lesson. On December 19, 2004, Violette, through Bryce Jr., arranged to meet Louie at the clubhouse to discuss the matter and see if it was true. After the meeting, Louie was intercepted speaking to Bryce Jr. about the clubhouse meeting with Violette.

"I thought I was gonna have to call you from the hospital there for a while," Louie told Jonathan Bryce. "Yeah. Fuck, I am still fuckin' sweatin' right now, man. I thought I was gonna get a fuckin' workin' over there."

That was still to come.

On January 20, 2005, Plante was asked to join Violette and Jonathan Bryce, who had arranged to meet Louie at night in a remote parking lot on Burnaby Mountain, in front of Horizons Restaurant, which is in a forested area just below Simon Fraser University.

---

* Glen Louie was never charged.

Earlier in the day, police listened as Violette called John Bryce, Sr., requesting a meeting in five minutes at Bryce's office. Police surveillance confirmed Violette going into Bryce's business, Hi-Way Choppers. After the meeting, Violette called Plante, telling him to meet him at the East End clubhouse.

Plante drove Violette and Jonathan Bryce to meet Louie. Once they got there, however, Violette took one look at the parking lot where they were supposed to meet and suggested it was too public—they didn't "wanna be fuckin' poundin' him out in the parkin' lot," Violette said, adding they would get Louie to stop halfway down the road.

Jonathan Bryce called Louie to clarify where they were supposed to meet. Louie arrived minutes later. Violette and Plante got out of the car and walked toward Louie's vehicle, which was parked about five feet away.

"Ah, I can't get out. Ah . . . ," Bryce Jr. was heard saying from the back seat—Violette had jumped out of the car without moving the seat forward so Bryce could get out. He eventually found the release and got out of the car.

As soon as Louie got out of his car, Violette slapped, punched and kicked him. Plante's listening device picked up the blows—and Louie's screams of pain.

"What I fuckin' tell ya about that, huh?" Violette yelled at Louie.

"Didn't do nothin'," Louie said.

"Huh? What the fuck?" Violette said, with a smacking sound heard in the background.

"I didn't do nothin'," Louie reiterated.

"Yeah, you fuckin' liar cocksucker," Violette said.

"Ow, fuck," Louie said. "Porno, I never said anything."

Louie stumbled and fell toward Violette, whose nickname was Porno. Plante tried pulling Louie back and they both fell. Plante would later say he was trying to protect Louie from further blows. Violette booted Louie while he was down. Jonathan Bryce also tried kicking Louie and inadvertently kicked Plante from behind.

Plante got up, but Louie stayed on the ground. He noticed blood on Louie's face. Just then, a vehicle coming from Horizons Restaurant slowed and passed. The man in the car looked at what was happening, then drove away. When the motorist was out of sight, he called 911.

"I didn't do it, Porno," Louie said.

"Fuck you, you didn't," the biker said. "Get up. I ain't done with you."

Violette demanded that Louie take off his belt and said, "You get the fuck outta town."

"You got the belt on right now?" Plante asked.

No, Louie said. He wasn't wearing any belt, causing his pants to fall down. Plante told Louie to pull his pants up.

"Well, when ya do . . . throw all your stuff in a bag and take it to the house," Plante sternly told Louie—meaning he was supposed to gather up any Hells Angels support gear he had and take it to the East End clubhouse.

"Okay," Louie said.

"Hey, I told ya, don't be talkin' to people like that," Violette warned. "I warned you about that."

"Throw all your stuff in a bag and call Jonathan," Plante told Louie again.

"And you know what, you better forget what happened," Violette warned, meaning Louie should never discuss what had just occurred.

As they drove away, Violette said that Louie was lucky to still be walking. He suggested Louie had been let off gently because of the car coming down the hill. The biker asked if anyone had blood on them—he was concerned about being stopped by the police.

"Bang, I nailed him, right?" Violette bragged to his cohorts during the drive back to the clubhouse. The biker mocked Louie for "crying like a baby" after being beaten.

Violette again told Jonathan Bryce he wanted all of Louie's Hells Angels support wear and to put the word out that he didn't want to see Louie with anyone connected to the club. Violette, Bryce and Plante then discussed what John Bryce Sr. knew about Louie using the Hells Angels name without permission. Violette said he had spoken with the chapter president that afternoon. Jonathan Bryce also confirmed that his father was aware of the situation, having also spoken to his dad earlier that day. His father was mad at Louie, he added.

Jonathan Bryce then bragged he had kicked Louie. Plante corrected him, telling him that he had actually received the kick. In a phone call intercepted by police 11 days later, Louie told Jonathan Bryce that he had been "pissin" blood ever since the beating.

Later that night, Plante complained to Punko about the poor performance of Jonathan Bryce Jr. in Louie's beating.

"That's not cool. Jonathan will be gone, he'll be gone for that," Punko said.

"He disgusted me, man," Plante said, pretending to be disappointed by Jonathan Bryce's inaction.

"This should be brought up, I'll tell, I'll talk to Porno about that. I'll say Jonathan should be gone," Punko suggested.

• • •

Four days later, on January 24, 2005, the chapter held its anniversary party. That night, Jonathan Bryce was promoted a step up in the Hells Angels program, becoming a "hangaround" and receiving his new flasher. Plante, however, was passed over for a promotion and remained at the beck and call of other chapter members.

Plante was furious. One East End member, Damiano Dipopolo, sent Plante on an errand that night. Plante left the clubhouse and never returned. He left his clubhouse keys on the windshield of the vehicle owned by "Tattoo Rob" Thomas, who lived in Kelowna.

"I'm done," Plante told his police handlers later that night.

Police tried to convince him it wasn't that important that he was passed over for promotion to a hangaround, but Plante couldn't get over it. He was tired and pissed off.

"It was his ego," one of the officers at the meeting with Plante that night recalled. But he also admitted Plante was worn down from the cumulative pressure of having to answer to his handlers and his Hells Angels bosses. It had finally taken its toll.

"He didn't have a life anymore," the Mountie conceded.

Police didn't have all the Hells Angels targets they had hoped for, but realized Plante was at the end of his rope. He was exhausted. Reluctantly, his handlers agreed to help him disappear.

Before Plante was relocated by police—he chose not to enter the witness protection program—he and his girlfriend were flown to Mexico for a holiday. "I'd always said when this investigation was over, I wanted to get away, I wanted to go to Mexico, I wanted to sit in the sun," Plante would later recall.

"Well, let's get away. Let's go somewhere," inspector Gary Shinkaruk, the team leader of the E-Pandora investigation told Plante. Police booked a two-week trip for Plante and his girlfriend to Cabo San Lucas, located at the tip of the Baja peninsula in Mexico.

"I didn't pick Cabo, I didn't pick anything. Gary took care of everything," Plante would recall.

The trip didn't start off well. Inspector Andy Richards and another officer, Brad Stephens, one of Plante's police handlers, were supposed to accompany Plante and his girlfriend to keep them safe in Mexico. As it turned out, Richards came down with the flu just before the flight to the United States, where they were to transfer planes to Cabo.

Once at the Vancouver airport, Plante and his girlfriend also had problems with their identification—Plante's girlfriend learned she was unable to travel to the United States, so she would have to fly directly to Mexico. And Plante had lost his identification—he had left his wallet in a rented truck at Christmas and it was never recovered.

By the time police sorted out the problems, the flight had already left with Stephens and his girlfriend on the plane. Plante's tickets were canceled and a new flight was booked for the next day. By that time, police learned it was going to take a week for Plante's girlfriend to sort out her problems—Plante would eventually have to pay for the new ticket for her—so Plante and Richards got on the plane.

Plante had never met Richards before, but learned Richards had spent years with the Vancouver police anti-biker squad, which had worked on one of the first successful Hells Angels investigations, Project Nova. This was the investigation that led to the convictions of Francisco Pires and Ronaldo Lising for cocaine trafficking.

During a 2002 raid on the Vancouver Hells Angels clubhouse in Coquitlam, police had found photos of members of their squad with their faces circled, including one of Richards. Another of the investigators, Brad Parker, had received threatening phone calls at his home.

"Stop what you're doing or you're going to get it," the first caller warned.

Five minutes later, another call was made by another person—the voice was younger sounding. The caller said: "You'd better fuckin' watch your back."

Parker, his wife and kids took security precautions, but there were no further problems. The Hells Angels denied they made the calls.

"We didn't do that," Hells Angels East End chapter president John Bryce told a *Vancouver Sun* reporter about the phone calls. "We don't want to have any problem with the police, right. So why would we do that? It's insane."

• • •

While in Mexico, Plante stayed at an all-inclusive resort. He was happy not to have to be watching over his shoulder for the Hells Angels. After a week, Plante's girlfriend joined him and Richards and Stephens flew home. They were replaced by two other E-Pandora officers, Stuart Priest and Gary Shinkaruk.

After the Mexico trip, Plante would only return to Vancouver under tight police protection to testify at a number of Hells Angels trials.

Members of the East End chapter immediately began to worry when they couldn't reach Plante. Initially, they thought he was sulking over getting thumped outside Brandi's and continued discussions about how to punish the guy who beat up Plante. But they soon realized Plante probably wasn't coming back. He seemed to have disappeared.

"Fucking goof rat," biker Rob Thomas was heard saying about Plante in a phone call to Punko, who said he wanted to beat Plante for a "fuckin' hour" if he found him.

On January 25, 2005, Punko met with Renaud and Ghavami to discuss Plante's disappearance. Neither man had heard from him. The discussion then turned to trying to make some money selling drugs, with Punko suggesting that Renaud could sell cocaine in Alberta for him. They also discussed, with police secretly listening via a bug in Punko's residence, continuing the methamphetamine production. Renaud said he already had a half barrel in production. "I already got it. Don't worry, I can sell it," he told Punko.

The biker suggested Ghavami could become a third partner, so he could make some money. Renaud suggested Ghavami could do the "running around" because Renaud didn't want to deal with "a million [Hells Angels] members."

"No, no, no. Nobody else knows about this," Punko said. "Well, guys know that you do that . . . Ronnie knows."

Punko went on to explain that "If someone comes in and leans on you . . . And if we get ripped off. Fuck, I'm gonna lose it, man. And fuck whoever ripped us off."

Ghavami asked Punko what he should do if Plante contacted him. Get Plante to come and talk to me, Punko said.

Four days later, Renaud and Ghavami met again at Punko's residence. The biker, getting worked up, said he was going to smash Plante's skull wide open if he saw him. If Plante shows up at the East End clubhouse, Punko said, he would grab the baseball bat behind the bar and crack him.

Around the same time, police wiretaps picked up Potts becoming concerned that Plante still had the cache of guns, silencers, grenades and dynamite that Potts had given him for safekeeping.

On January 27, 2005, police intercepted a phone call between David Giles and Stanley Gillis, the sergeant at arms of the East End chapter. Gillis informed Giles that it appeared Plante had left the club.

About an hour later, Giles was seen meeting David Revell of Kelowna at a Tim Hortons coffee shop in Abbotsford. The two men then drove in Revell's pickup truck to Trev Deeley Motorcycles, the Harley-Davidson dealer in Vancouver. They later went to the East End clubhouse, where they were observed standing outside, talking to John Bryce. From there, they went to

Bryce's business, Hi-Way Choppers, located at 3750 Parker Street in Burnaby, where the three men went inside.

Revell later got in his vehicle and met Giles for a bite to eat at the now-defunct Admiral Pub at 4125 Hastings Street in Burnaby. After that, Revell drove his truck on the freeway, Highway 1, heading toward Kelowna.

After no word of Plante for more than two months, Potts phoned Plante's buddy, Nima Ghavami, on March 31, 2005, to see if he had heard anything. Potts was worried that Plante still had the bag of guns and other weapons and was concerned that other East End members would start asking questions about the arsenal.

"Yeah, I need to get him a message through that um, you know, like [clears throat] nobody's been asking about him, right," Potts said over the phone.

"Yeah," Ghavami said.

"Nobody really cares, right?" Potts said. "But at some point I have to tell everybody that he took off with that big black, uh, bag, that box of things."

"Yeah," Ghavami said.

"That don't belong to me," Potts continued. "Is there any way you can leave him a message from me to uh, to say that uh, you know like, hey, buddy, like, you should call your friend because he doesn't know what to do about the, the bag of tools, you know."

Potts added: "Just tell him I'm going to be in trouble, you know, if he doesn't make arrangements to return it to me, right?"

"Yeah, okay," Ghavami responded.

"I'm gonna have to tell everybody," Potts added, which police took to mean he would be forced to tell other Hells Angels members that Plante had the cache of weapons. "He'll know who everybody is. It doesn't belong to me ... And right now nobody cares where he is, but then they all will, right?"

Ghavami agreed.

"Everybody'll be looking for him then," Potts explained. "Yeah, yeah, yeah, tell him, and say if he doesn't wanna call us, maybe call the lawyer, and uh, make arrangements with him."

"Okay," Ghavami said.

"You know, if he doesn't want to call us, like, call somebody. You know, like, that he feels good about, right?"

Potts added: "I have no problem with him at all... If I'm not gonna hear from him ever again, I need those things back."

"Okay. Sounds good," Ghavami said.

"Alright, an' just be friendly with him, and try to make him come forward," Potts said.

In the days that followed, police listened to some guarded references by Hells Angels members to "our missing friend" and speculation about where he had gone. It would be months before they would learn the truth.

CHAPTER 6

The K-Town Crew

Aggravation caused by Plante's disappearance began to fade after a few days. The police wiretaps began tracing discussions about East End members setting up a new Hells Angels chapter in Kelowna, located on Okanagan Lake in the interior of B.C.

The city was one of the fastest-growing in the province as people flocked to enjoy the beautiful sandy beaches, boating, abundant golf courses, fruit orchards, vineyards and desert-like summer heat. The bikers wanted to take advantage of the booming drug trade in the scenic city that served as a summer playground for wealthy city folks from Vancouver and Alberta.

Using information gathered by Plante, police asked a judge to authorize an electronic listening device to eavesdrop on secret meetings inside the East End Hells Angels clubhouse in Kelowna, located at 837 Ellis Avenue. The bug was covertly installed in the clubhouse by an RCMP unit known as Special I, which specializes in installing listening devices. Members of the covert unit surreptitiously enter a residence or business of the target and install one or more "bugs" that can be monitored by police. Conversations are recorded digitally with someone assigned to monitor conversations and take notes, summarizing the conversations, especially mentions of targets of the investigation.

One conversation recorded by police through the Kelowna clubhouse bug captured David Giles discussing the possibility of establishing a separate chapter in Kelowna, where a number of then-Hells Angels members owned homes: Hans Kuth, Carlos Verna, Michael (Speedy) Christiansen, Damiano Dipopolo, Lloyd "Louie" Robinson (who has since retired from the Angels), Richard Goldammer, Guy Rossignol, Bruce Skreptak and Robert Thomas, a Kelowna tattoo-shop owner who at the time was a prospect but later became a full-patch member.

It takes six members to establish a new Hells Angels chapter, which must be sponsored by another chapter. In this case, the East End would sponsor the proposed Kelowna chapter. The conversation also became more general, and at one point Giles could be heard pounding the table with his fist and exhorting other members to do everything they could to benefit the motorcycle club. He also made it clear during the meeting that the club had a certain exclusivity and notoriety, which other people would try to use for their own personal gain or benefit.

This recording from January 24, 2005, which provided a rare glimpse into the inner circle of the East End chapter of the Hells Angels, is believed to mark the first time that police in B.C. penetrated a meeting of the notorious biker group.

Giles joined the East End Hells Angels in 1995, after leaving a chapter in Sherbrooke, Quebec. At the time of his speech, he had been a Hells Angel for more than 20 years. He had been through the biker wars with the rival Rock Machine biker gang in Quebec that claimed more than 100 lives.

"Ten years in Montreal, two wars, huh, that's enough of that," police overheard him saying one day. Some police suspected Giles might still have solid Mafia connections from his Montreal days.

During the clubhouse meeting, Giles talked about how members who had moved to Kelowna were having to commute to Vancouver for weekly East End chapter meetings, traveling up to 1,000 kilometers a month. "We're not gonna leave the East End, we're gonna separate from the East End with the same motto, with the same rules, with the same functions in mind," Giles explained.

He admitted he was tired of driving to Vancouver to attend meetings. But he could live with a new chapter not being established, he added.

"I can just as easy stay in my house and drive back and forth . . . and get along just nicely," he said.

But as things stood at the time, too many people were coming to the Kelowna clubhouse looking to gain something from the reputation of the Hells Angels, he said.

"For me," Giles said, "there isn't one fuckin' citizen out there, not one that I socialize with, talk to or have anything to do with, that [isn't thinking] 'What can I get from him?' "

Giles said the question for each biker should be: "What's he gonna do for me that's gonna benefit this house? . . . And that's how I feel everybody should think. 'Cause this ain't about what it can do for you; it's supposed to be what you can do for the club."

It seemed to be an odd twist on the famous 1961 inaugural speech by U.S. president John F. Kennedy, when he told Americans: "And so, my fellow Americans: ask not what your country can do for you—ask what you can do for your country . . . ask not what America will do for you, but what together we can do for the freedom of man."

Giles, however, didn't have such lofty goals as the freedom of man. This was about the freedom of the Hells Angels to take care of business. Giles went on to say that "in no way shape or form should anybody be riding on that notoriety, on our coattails. Period. And it's happening all the time. And I'm not gonna tolerate it. Period. A few people around this town are going to be told."

He told his fellow bikers at the Kelowna clubhouse to think about electing executive officers. He said he was working with members of the East End chapter "to convince them how to feel comfortable with what we wanna do, and then go forward."

The wiretap also picked up Rob Thomas, a Hells Angels prospect, seeking guidance on the need to work with the demands of the recruitment program. Thomas ran a Kelowna tattoo parlor but was finding it difficult to keep steady hours when he was scheduled to be at the East End clubhouse in Vancouver.

Giles pointed out that another prospect, Jonathan Bryce Jr., was at the clubhouse every day, so Thomas had to make an effort to be at the clubhouse three days a week to tell Jonathan what needed to be done. Giles also advised Thomas to bring his concerns "to the table" at weekly meetings. Giles added he would remind East End members that Thomas would be representing "the club" at an upcoming tattoo convention in Vancouver.

Days later, police listened to a phone conversation between Giles and a Kelowna woman named Sherry Shagwell, who called Giles to complain she had received threatening phone messages from a man named John Ryder. She explained Ryder mentioned he was connected to "your club" in his phone messages. Giles assured Shagwell he would "get things straightened out."

An hour later, Giles phoned Ryder. Giles identified himself as "Gyrator from East End Hells Angels," explaining "the club name has been used here, which I really don't like." He asked Ryder to return Shagwell's property.

Less than 20 minutes later, Ryder called Giles, saying the situation had been taken care of. He apologized to Giles for the "hassle," a clear demonstration of the power of the Hells Angels patch.

Shagwell then called Giles minutes later, thanking him for dealing with Ryder. "I told him not to be using the [Hells Angels] name again, and for you the same thing," Giles advised.

• • •

Police learned that Giles was very wary about talking on phones and preferred meeting people in person. Another undercover police unit, known as Special O, was undertaking physical surveillance of targets. The unit watched Giles meeting people outside gyms, restaurants and gas stations.

Special O officers are asked to dress to look like average folks, not cops. Usually several cars will follow a target, so if the person being followed turns into a parking lot, the car directly behind will carry on and another will turn in and adapt to the situation—getting out of the car and going into a restaurant, for example, where they will sit near the target and try to eavesdrop on their conversation.

On January 28, 2005, police also listened to a call by Giles, when he told David Roger Revell not to say anything—it was a veiled conversation. Giles, who said he was at the Kelowna clubhouse, agreed to meet Revell at a nearby gas station on Spall Road.

A few days later, on February 3, 2005, Giles was overheard telling Revell: "That's enough on the fuckin' telephone. I'll talk to ya when I get home."

And around the same time Revell told Giles: "Sometime today I need to have a little chat with you." Giles agreed to meet after he met with "Skreppy," a reference to another Hells Angels member, Bruce Skreptak.

Revell, whose nickname was Baldy, was a big man with a shaved head. His frequent contact with Giles attracted the attention of police, who learned that Revell ran a number of businesses in the Kelowna area at the time: Reflex Gym, the Sunrise Family Bar & Grill, the Washtub Laundromat and a used-car lot called Westside Truck Auto & Pawn. The businesses were all in Westbank, located on the other side of Okanagan Lake from Kelowna. At the time a floating bridge connected the two cities, although Westbank was a smaller, more rural town.

Another man who came to police attention was Richard Andrew Rempel, who worked at Revell's car lot. He lived in a room in the back of the dealership office. Giles and Revell also lived in Westbank, which overlooks Okanagan Lake.

Police listened in as Giles discussed a matter with his common-law partner. She complained that Giles had put $500 worth of WestJet airline tickets on her credit card for Revell to fly to Calgary. (Police surveillance observed Revell and Rempel going together on the trip from Kelowna's airport. Revell was carrying a black carry-on bag and talking on his cell phone as he boarded the plane.)

Giles explained to his partner that Revell "went there to make money for me," adding, "He made me 30 grand in the past few months." This conversation took place February 14, 2005.

Two days later, Revell called Giles, telling him he was going to see "our buddy from the north" and "that's all good." Another two days went by, then Revell called Giles again, saying he was going to Vancouver to see "Bully"—Hells Angels member Guy Rossignol—and suggested setting aside a couple of days so they could go north to discuss a matter " 'cause I know that he deals with one o' your guys up there."

Two days later, Revell asked Giles over the phone what the "deal" is. "Three," Giles said. Revell asked where it was because he didn't recall. "I'll tell ya later," Giles responded. Later in the day, Giles was overheard telling Revell the meeting was set for 3 p.m. Revell had Giles confirm "the only rules is that you gave—this guy doesn't get hit there."

Once Giles returned home from Vancouver, Revell asked how his trip went. "Good. No bad news is good news," Giles said. "Covered your ass for ya." Revell thanked him.

· · ·

About a month later, on March 17, video surveillance recorded Rempel gaining access to storage locker F-11 at Westbank Self-Storage at 2231 Moose Road. The video showed Rempel unlocking two padlocks, entering the locker and leaving a minute later carrying a dark duffel bag, which he put down on the step to lock the door's padlocks. He got into his car with the bag and drove off.

Video surveillance cameras also recorded Rempel entering the storage locker on April 2, 2005. He arrived in an Intrepid, which he parked in front of locker F-11. He crawled into the back seat and, about a minute later, got out of the rear passenger door.

Rempel left the car door ajar, unfastened the padlocks on the locker, returned to the car and retrieved a blue gym bag with black handles. He put the bag in the locker, emerging a few seconds later empty-handed. Rempel locked the padlocks, got into the Intrepid and drove away about two minutes after he arrived.

Two days later, on April 4 at 1:04 p.m., the police surveillance team observed Rempel and Revell's son, John, at the front gate of the self-storage units. Rempel pulled the Intrepid beside the Chevy pickup's driver's side window, and he and John Revell chatted. After two minutes, Revell drove his truck into the self-storage compound, followed by Rempel. An access card was used to enter the gates of the compound.

Rempel was recorded on video surveillance accessing locker F-11, which he unlocked and opened. He entered the locker empty-handed. Less than a minute later, he emerged from the locker with his left arm clasped tightly against his body. He locked the locker door and returned to the Intrepid holding his left arm tightly against his body.

That evening, just after 8 p.m. the police executed a warrant to search the locker. Police seized two bags inside. The first was a blue No Boundaries bag with black handles and sides. It contained three separate one-kilogram bricks of cocaine in sealed plastic bags. There were also two empty plastic bags the same size, which appeared to have each held a one-kilogram brick of cocaine. The second bag was a smaller gym bag containing a Panther brand stun gun and a .25-caliber Jennings handgun inside a blue box.

The next morning, April 5, 2005, there was a series of text messages sent between the BlackBerry phones of Revell and Rempel, who were still completely in the dark about the locker having been raided by police the previous day.

The undercover police surveillance team observed Rempel driving the Intrepid to Revell's Sunrise Café. Revell arrived before 9 a.m. driving his blue Ford F350 pickup truck. Both men went inside briefly and were seen leaving together minutes later. Later that morning, both men were observed at the car lot on Ross Road, where Rempel was observed removing the licence plates from the Intrepid.

Just after noon that day, Giles phoned Revell and asked if he had a fax machine. Giles arrived minutes later at Revell's

Reflex Gym on Brown Road, holding some papers. They stood together in the parking lot, talking.

Minutes later, Giles drove his truck to the car lot on Ross Road and had it washed. Giles was wearing a white sweatshirt with "AFFA" ("Angels Forever, Forever Angels") emblazoned across the chest.

About two hours later, police followed Revell as he pulled into a Chevron gas station on Highway 97 in Kelowna. He stopped in the middle of the lot and waited. Two minutes later, a red Honda arrived and parked next to Revell. The driver of the Honda was an East Indian drug dealer named Shingara Bassi. Revell got out of his truck and chatted briefly with Bassi. The two men shook hands, returned to their vehicles and drove off.

The next morning, April 6, 2005, Revell sent a text message to Rempel: "Brown guy needs one. Wayting 4 him now." They were both using BlackBerry phones to send text messages.

Police surveillance observed Rempel going to the Intrepid parked at the car lot. He entered the car through the front driver's side door and leaned into the back seat, appearing to manipulate something in the back. Rempel got out of the car through the front passenger's side door, with his left arm held closely to his body. He walked back to the office and opened the door with his right hand, with his left arm still held up against his body. He had a glove on his right hand, even though the weather was not cold.

The next morning at 9:42 a.m., Revell sent a text message to Rempel: "U up?"

"Ya, I'm ready," Rempel texted back. The police watched him go to the green Intrepid, which was parked in front of the office. He went in the car for 10 seconds, then returned to the office. At the same time, Revell was observed leaving the Sunrise Restaurant.

"I'm going to go up to Sun and grab some food. I can't find either of those things," Rempel said.

"I have them," Revell replied in his text message. "I will need u in 20 min."

"Do I have time to eat?" Rempel asked by e-mail.

"No. give me 5," Revell replied. "Open gate."

Rempel, wearing a camouflage-style jacket, walked out of the office and opened the car lot gate.

"Brown Chad needs the same kind as last time," Revell responded. "U have it thair or storage?"

"Storage I think," Rempel responded. "I could check here. I'm not sure what we got where."

Revell replied: "Have a look [there]. And if u have it I will send him now."

Surveillance observed Rempel at the car lot with a shovel. Minutes later, Rempel sent a text message to Revell, saying: "Not here."

Four minutes later, Revell's son John arrived at the car lot in his truck. Rempel was seen entering the office, then John Revell drove out of the lot.

Revell sent a text message to Rempel, asking him to "Get one of those out and have a look at one."

Rempel came out of the office and got into the driver's side of the Intrepid, leaving the door open. He then opened the rear driver's side door, leaning into the back seat. Two minutes later he backed out of the car and stood up with his left arm held tightly against his body. He closed the rear driver's side door with his right hand and returned to the office, keeping his left arm against his body.

Rempel sent a message to Revell: "It's soft but really shiny, good color."

"He is on his way," Revell replied.

"Is he gonna wanna look at this?" Rempel asked. "Ya," Revell responded, "so keep one out. Leave the rest in the car."

At 11:13 a.m., Bassi arrived at the car lot driving the same red Honda that the surveillance police had observed the previous day. Bassi got out of the car and approached the office, carrying a small, empty orange gym bag. Bassi knocked on the door and he went into the office. Four minutes later, Bassi left the office carrying the same orange gym bag, which now by its bulk appeared to contain something, and got back into the red Honda.

"Brown guy just left," Rempel texted Revell.

Police followed the Honda from the car lot. It headed northbound on Highway 97 into Kelowna. When the police car activated its lights and siren, the Honda turned abruptly into the parking lot of Kelowna Senior Secondary School and came to sudden halt. Bassi bolted, carrying a duffel bag, and began running across Richter Street toward a Petro-Canada gas station. Police chased and caught him, seizing a dark blue duffel bag containing the orange gym bag. A one-kilogram brick of cocaine was inside.

At 11:18 a.m. that morning, sergeant Al Haslett of the RCMP, pretending he was an employee of Westside Self-Storage, called Revell's Reflex Gym, leaving a message for "Richard" (Rempel) to call about his locker.

What followed was a further flurry of text messages between Revell and Rempel, expressing concern about the phone call. Revell sent a text message to Rempel, saying someone had called "about your locker. That's not good." Revell told him to call the guy at the self-storage company and "c wat they want." He texted Rempel the number to call.

Rempel responded immediately, speculating that the storage locker staff were probably looking for the "storage key" and that he would have to bring back the key that he had given to Revell.

"Call them now and make sure," Revell's message said.

Minutes later, Rempel sent back a message: "My locker got robbed."

"U r fucking kidding. Someone is watching u," Revell replied.

"I guess so. Fuck, who?" Rempel asked.

Revell and Rempel messaged back and forth, discussing who might be watching, who might have broken into the locker and what Rempel should say to the staff at Westside Self-Storage.

Revell suggested that Rempel should look at the security video surveillance at the compound to get an idea of who was responsible for the break-in. In another message, Revell told Rempel: "We need to go [and] bury those now"—meaning the cocaine at the car lot.

"Where should we put them?" Rempel asked.

"Don't know, someone is watching u." Revell replied.

Rempel suggested it would be a good idea to leave the car "all locked up . . . we can keep an eye on it." He added: "No one knows about the locker." Revell responded "Ya maybe."

" 'Cause if watching they will c where I go," Rempel added in another text message.

"Ya, fuck. Who is watching u?" Revell pondered.

"The only person I can think of is Mitch," Rempel replied by text.

Revell: "Does he no [know] about locker?"

Rempel: "I never told him but he knows what I'm involved in, sorta, and he knows a lot of pieces of shit. All he would have to do is follow me around a bit."

Revell: "He has no car. And I don't think he's that stupid."

"Ya maybe," Rempel replied. "All he would have to do is tell his buddies who to follow."

"U think he would do that?" Revell asked.

"I don't know. He tried before," Rempel replied. "I'm going to grab some food. I can't figure this out."

Police watched as Rempel left the car lot office and walked to the Intrepid. He opened the driver's side door and stuck his head and torso in the vehicle for about 30 seconds, all the while keeping an eye on a man—an undercover surveillance officer—looking at cars for sale. Rempel then left the car and returned to the office. After the man left the lot, Rempel left the office, closed the gate and walked northbound on Ross Road toward the Sunrise Family Bar & Grill, located at the Comfort Inn.

Just after noon, Revell sent a text message, instructing Rempel to "Put plates on car. I need u."

"I'm at the restaurant," Rempel responded.

Revell said that he needed Rempel in 15 minutes. Rempel replied: "I will be as quick as I can."

Ten minutes later, Revell told Rempel to "get car" and "head 2 glenrosa."

"I haven't eaten yet," Rempel responded.

"Hurry," Revell replied.

"I'm just leaving restaurant now," Rempel texted 12 minutes later.

"Head 2 motorhome," Revell said in a text message. "Where r u?"

"Just leaving lot," Rempel replied. Police watched as he locked the gate behind him and headed west on Highway 97.

"Watch your mirrors," Revell warned.

"Where u now?" Revell asked by text a few minutes later.

"Leaving w[est]bank," Rempel replied. Three minutes later, he sent another message: "By mill," a reference to the Gorman's lumber mill, a local landmark and one of the biggest employers in the area.

Surveillance police following Rempel lost sight of him as he turned off the highway. But other police were tailing Revell as he drove at high speed along Glenrosa, a winding country road near Gorman's mill. Another undercover officer finally caught sight of Rempel in the Intrepid and picked up the tail.

"I'm here," Rempel texted to Revell, who instructed Rempel to take the plates off the car. "K," Rempel replied.

Revell picked up Rempel in his truck, which was spotted racing back toward Westbank along Glenrosa Road, past Gorman's Mill and to the parking lot of the Reflex Gym in Westbank.

About an hour later, Rempel was recorded on video surveillance at Westbank Self-Storage, examining locker F-11 with two other people. At 2:29 p.m. Rempel sent a text message to Revell, reporting that the staff would not let him see the security videotapes.

At 2:45 p.m., police found the Intrepid parked next to two motor homes on a property at 3230 Preston Road, Westbank. One of the motor homes was registered to Revell. The hood of the Intrepid was still hot, indicating it had recently been driven. The car had no licence plates. By the vehicle identification number, police believed the registered owner was Curtis Helle.

Seventeen minutes later, a man named Mike DeMattos arrived at 3230 Preston Road in a black truck. I own the property, he told police. I rent it to a car lot business in Westbank. Then he left.

DeMattos obviously contacted Revell, who discussed this new development in a series of text messages to Rempel.

"We have a prob," Revell texted.

"What?" Rempel replied.

"Cops at car where we just took it."

"Fuck fuck fuck," Rempel texted. "What do we do?"

"Tell buddy that is reg 2 say nothing," Revell suggested.

At 3:25 p.m., DeMattos returned again to 3230 Preston Road, telling the police that the car was not stolen. He provided the officer with a business card with the name of Kris Hoely and a phone number. After explaining that this was the person who owned the car, DeMattos departed a second time.

"Were they marked [police cars] or undercovers?" Rempel texted.

"Don't know," Revell replied.

Minutes later, police watched Revell meeting DeMattos outside the Dairy Queen, next to the Reflex Gym.

Revell and Rempel then exchanged text messages, suggesting they concoct a story to try to distract the police, try to convince the police that the Intrepid was not stolen, so they would leave it alone. Revell asked Rempel for the full name of "Curtis" and Rempel replied that it was "Curtis Hellie"—Helle was the correct spelling.

"Y?" Rempel asked.

"Cops r saying car is stollin," Revell replied. "Where is Curt?"

"Here," Rempel replied. Revell suggested Curtis should speak to the police about the Intrepid, explaining he owned the car and was hiding it from his ex-wife.

"What was cop's name this morn?" Revell asked.

"Is written down on the yellow piece of paper at the gym," Rempel replied.

Revell drove his truck from the Dairy Queen and pulled into the parking lot of Reflex Gym. He walked into the gym wearing black sweat pants and a grey sleeveless shirt. After finding the name of the cop who was supposedly investigating the locker break-in, and comparing it to the name of the cop at the property where the Intrepid was parked, Revell suddenly realized it was the same officer.

"Same cop. they broke into locker," Revell texted to Rempel. "They r watching u and me."

"The cops did it?" Rempel replied. "Cock suckers."

At 3:40 p.m. DeMattos returned for a third time to his property where the Intrepid had been stashed. Police told him they would be obtaining search warrants for the car and the motor home in connection with a drug investigation. DeMattos said he understood and that he just wanted to know what to tell the owners. One of the officers gave DeMattos a business card.

At 4 p.m., Revell was observed meeting with Giles in the parking lot of the Reflex Gym. Minutes later, both men left the parking lot in separate vehicles.

Police tailed Rempel, who was driving a Mercury Grand Marquis out of a driveway on Sexsmith Road, later determined as Helle's address. Curtis Helle, the alleged registered owner of the vehicle, was in the front passenger seat.*

Revell sent several messages to Rempel, telling him to take Helle "to the car" and that Helle should arrive "by himself... let him take the car."

"Okay," Rempel responded, adding he first had to fill up the car with gas. Police observed Rempel pull the Grand Marquis into a Super Save station, just north of the intersection of Highway 97 and Highway 33. Helle was wearing a baseball cap.

At 4:10 p.m., Revell arrived at 3230 Preston Road in his truck at high speed. He was aggressive and agitated. He told police they were on private property and demanded they produce a search warrant. The police explained they were involved in a drug investigation and intended to seize the Intrepid and the motor home registered in Revell's name. Revell said he would take the motor home unless the police showed him a search warrant.

You do that and you'll be arrested, police warned. Pointing to an officer's pepper spray, Revell said "That's not going to work... it does not work on me." Revell got back in his truck and gave the cops the finger as he drove off at high speed.

At 4:26 p.m., police stopped the Grand Marquis and arrested Rempel and Helle; although Helle was questioned, he was later released without being charged.

---

* Helle was never charged.

Police seized a BlackBerry found next to the driver's seat. One of the officers removed the battery and memory card from the BlackBerry to prevent remote erasure. The device was later sent for analysis and the text messages were downloaded. Although the user name was "Greg Murphy," Rempel never disputed he was the person who had been sending text messages on the phone.

Minutes later, police stopped Revell's pickup truck and arrested him. Police seized a BlackBerry from a pocket in the front console of the truck.

Later that evening, police obtained search warrants for various locations. One was executed at Revell's car lot. Inside the office, police seized numerous Ziploc baggies, a can of bear spray and papers in the name of Rempel, found in the bedroom at the back of the office.

In the living room, police found an electronic security card and three keys in a leather jacket. The keys were found to open storage locker F-11 at Westside Self-Storage, while the card opened the entry gate to the compound. Also seized was a black Hells Angels "support gear" hoody from a loveseat in the living room. In the bathroom, police seized an electronic scale, various clear plastic bags, several vacuum-sealed bags that had been opened, and an Exacto knife.

Police also searched the exterior of the property for drugs that might have been buried with a shovel that was located at the back of the building. A white plastic shopping bag containing a box of Ziploc baggies and several chunks of cocaine was found buried under about a foot of dirt in an area next to a barbecue. A white plastic shopping bag containing cocaine residue was also buried in the dirt along the fence line on the southeast corner of the property. More empty white shopping bags were found.

Police searched the Intrepid at 11 p.m. that evening, finding a hidden compartment between the back seat and the trunk that was secured by a magnetic lock fixed to the backrest. Inside the compartment, police found a blue No Boundaries duffel bag with black handles containing five individually packaged one-kilogram bricks of cocaine. The licence plates for the car were found in the trunk.

That evening, a Hells Angels member, Marcello Carlo Verna, advised Giles of Revell's arrest and the searches of Revell's car lot and gym. A wiretap caught Giles calling Revell's common-law partner, leaving a message for her to call him.

She called Giles at 11:04 p.m., saying Revell is "visiting the boys in blue." She told Giles that she'd spoken to a lawyer. Giles warned her that their phones were probably all "wired"—"yours, mine, all of them," but he didn't care. He said someone had come by to see him and informed him that police had raided Revell's car lot and gym.

"Let me know what, if any change or if he comes home or whatever," Giles told her.

The next morning, April 7, 2005, after Revell was released from custody, he phoned Giles but reached his common-law partner. Giles was out hiking, which was a part of his morning routine. Revell asked if Giles had his cell phone with him. He did. Revell immediately phoned Giles on his cell phone and arranged to meet him at his truck after he finished his hike.

Three days later, police listened as Revell told Giles that things were "absolutely fucking horrible. I hate my fucking life." Revell said he wanted to swing by Giles' house to discuss it. Giles and Revell continued having meetings and discussions until July, when they were both charged.

On May 2, at 6:13 p.m., Giles and Revell had a lengthy conversation that was secretly recorded via the wiretap in Giles' home. Police believed the two men were discussing the aftermath of the drug seizure.

The conversation began with Revell dropping by while Giles and his partner were watching a movie, *Meet the Fockers*. The two men moved to another room for more privacy, when Revell told Giles that he "paid $106,000."

"Well, what do we owe them?" Giles asked.

"Still owe 'em one-forty," Revell replied. Police would later allege it was a reference to $140,000.

Why, Giles asked Revell, who replied that he had "lost eight."

"Thought ya said he was going to forget costs," Giles said.

"No, he said costs of the eight, is what he told me," Revell explained.

"We'll get back up," Giles said.

On May 24, 2005, police listened as Giles asked a person named Mark Hilts if he had seen Baldy. Hilts replied that he had spoken to him briefly but he was trying to keep his distance from him. Hilts explained that the owner of the "property" where "the car" was found is "fuckin' livid" because the "cops dragged him in" for questioning.

"How many units do you usually put in the car?" Hilts asked.

"Seven," Giles replied.

Hilts explained that police said they found four units in the car. He wondered why the police would lie about the number of units found.

"I think it is time for me to have a chat with him," Giles said. "He lied to me."

When Giles, Revell and Rempel went to trial, the Crown would contend that these conversations linked Revell and Giles together in the cocaine business, showing Giles had knowledge of how many kilos of cocaine were kept in the Intrepid.

The defense, however, would make vigorous arguments to the contrary, but that was years away.

CHAPTER 7

The Roundup

The two-year joint-forces investigation involving the RCMP, Vancouver police and Combined Special Forces Unit of B.C., code-named Project E-Pandora, came to a conclusion on July 15, 2005, when police began rounding up the bikers and their associates.

A total of 19 men would eventually be charged, including eight full-patch Hells Angels, the son of East End chapter president John Bryce, and 10 associates. The serious charges included assault, extortion, possession and trafficking of illegal drugs, and possession of illegal weapons, including automatic handguns, silencers, grenades, dynamite with detonation cords and blasting caps.

During the investigation, police seized more than 20 kilograms of cocaine, more than 70 kilograms of marijuana, more than $200,000 in Canadian currency and 25 kilograms of methylamine, a precursor compound used to make the illegal "club drug" ecstasy.

Police also executed a series of search warrants on the homes of several senior bikers and associates in Vancouver and Kelowna.

Members of the public witnessed firsthand the police crackdown when heavily armed officers descended on the East End Hells Angels clubhouse at 3598 East Georgia, a quiet tree-lined residential street near Vancouver's eastern boundary. Police used a pickup truck with a battering ram on the back to smash down the fortified door of the clubhouse. The clubhouse was a veritable fortress with extremely sophisticated security measures: bullet-proof windows, steel doors with electronic numeric keypad locks, external motion-detector cameras, privacy fences and security cameras monitored 24 hours a day. A six-foot cedar fence ran along the property, except at the rear where there were two sliding gates. In the yard a camera was mounted on a light post 30 feet up, with commercial-style lighting aimed at the Kootenay Street side of the house.

The heavy front door was locked by two dead bolts and a metal handle. The entrance led to the lower floor of the house, which had a gym and a bar. There were five video monitors above the bar, showing the view caught by each of the exterior security cameras. On the upper floor was a kitchen area, where the windows had outside metal shutters that could be closed from the inside.

During the search, police found a metal briefcase marked "Porno"—the nickname of Hells Angels member Jean Joseph Violette. The briefcase contained copyright agreements signed by some of the full-patch members of the East End chapter.

Two Hells Angels were inside when police began battering down the door, causing the bikers to get on their cell phones. Minutes later, chapter president John Bryce showed up, looking angry.

"They just barged right in and knocked the door down," Bryce told *Vancouver Sun* reporter Amy O'Brian at the time. "We're not armed. We don't have weapons." He added: "They're looking for pictures of us. . . . They're just gathering information. That's what they do."

Bryce suggested the raid was probably tied to the fact that the Hells Angels had recently called then Vancouver police chief Jamie Graham a "windbag" after the chief had labeled the Hells Angels a criminal organization. The biker also complained that the two Hells Angels members inside the clubhouse offered to let police in, but instead police used battering rams to knock five metal doors off their frames.

Vancouver police constable Howard Chow later responded to Bryce's complaints, saying the police were justified in using force to break down the doors. "Despite their claims, I doubt that if we had sent a telegram saying that we were going to show up that they'd have the doors open to us, welcoming us with tea and crumpets," Chow said. "We did what was necessary to ensure the safety of everyone involved."

Another Hells Angels member, Robert Thomas, was also at the scene during the clubhouse raid. He put his hands on his hips and glared at police and the reporters who converged on the scene. Reporters didn't realize at the time, but a similar search was taking place at the East End chapter's satellite clubhouse in Kelowna, located at 837 Ellis Street.

Neighbors living in the area of the East Vancouver Hells Angels clubhouse told reporters at the time of the bust that they enjoyed having the bikers on their street, because they felt they provided a degree of safety. "They're good neighbors. We want them to stick around," one woman said.

Police found plenty of photos of Hells Angels members in the East End clubhouse in Vancouver, along with other Hells Angels paraphernalia. A sign near the bar read: "East End House of Pain." Another said: "What you do here, what you say here, stays here."

•   •   •

The raid on the clubhouse was just a part of the operation. Police already had the cache of guns Plante was holding for Potts, including four live grenades, a .45-caliber Colt semiautomatic pistol, an Intratec 9-mm semiautomatic pistol, a Ruger .22-caliber semiautomatic rifle, a Franchi .22-caliber semiautomatic rifle, a Voere bolt-action rifle and a Ruger .44 Magnum revolver. Police alleged the weapons cache was part of the Hells Angels arsenal; they were also executing search warrants at homes of Hells Angels members and seizing other guns.

At the home of Hells Angels member Jean Violette, police found a fanny pack containing two firearms in his office: a fully loaded .25-caliber Beretta model 20 handgun with a clip containing eight cartridges (the chamber was empty) and an unloaded Ruger model SP 101 revolver. Police also found a box of 50 soft-point .357 Magnum bullets. Violette did not have a licence for the weapons.

John Punko was arrested in his vehicle at Marlborough and Kingsway in Burnaby. A search warrant was executed at his residence, where four items were seized: a Smith & Wesson 9-mm handgun with a clip of bullets found on the master bedroom floor next to the bed; a brown fanny pack, containing a 9-mm magazine with bullets also found on the floor by the bed; a "Royal Sovereign" money-counting machine found inside a box in a spare bedroom; and a Hells Angels vest with "colors" found hanging in the master bedroom closet.

Discovered in the master bedroom of Ronaldo Lising's home was a safe containing a fanny pack with a loaded prohibited firearm—a .357-caliber Rossi M877 revolver, which contained six bullets. The fanny pack contained a plastic bag with another 15 rounds of ammunition.

Found in another fanny pack in the top drawer of a dresser in a basement room of Lising's home was a loaded .380-caliber Walther PPK/S semiautomatic pistol that had one bullet in the chamber and a loaded magazine; three loose bullets; and two more magazines for the pistol, each containing six bullets. Lising did not have a licence for either gun.

On closer inspection, the loaded Walther was found on top of a piece of paper containing information about the vehicles driven by Parminder Gill, his telephone numbers, and other information indicating that Gill "is on the move" and "has not showered or changed his clothes." Police also seized a BlackBerry that was later found to have text messages with a man named Leroy Serra Pereira, indicating Pereira had tried finding Gill through his wife's boutique.

Also in the basement of Lising's home, police discovered body armor and what appeared to be an "abduction kit" in a bag—a black balaclava, gloves, walkie-talkies and plastic "zap straps" used for makeshift handcuffs. Finally, police found a book on firearm silencers, a butterfly knife, small flares and a pen gun with .22-caliber bullets.

"We've taken a bunch of members into custody and we're hoping to charge them with a number of offenses—drugs, violence, weapons, explosives and criminal organization," said inspector Bob Paulson of the RCMP, who was at the time in charge of major investigations involving outlaw motorcycle gangs in B.C.

The bust was hailed as the largest roundup of Hells Angels members and their associates in B.C. history. The following Monday, police held a news conference to show the media some of the weapons and drugs seized during the investigation.

"Take a good, hard look at the table in front of you," constable Cam Kowalski of the RCMP's Outlaw Motorcycle Gang Squad told reporters. "Is that something that a gentleman's motorcycle club or any club would reasonably possess?" The outcome of the raid was that 19 men were charged with various offenses.

David Francis Giles, 56, a full-patch member of the East End chapter, was charged with possession of cocaine for the purpose of trafficking and commission of the offense in association with a criminal organization, "to wit, the East End Hells Angels."

Pursuant to the Criminal Code, anyone who commits a crime for the benefit of, at the direction of, or in association with a criminal organization can be sentenced to up to 14 years in prison over and above the sentence received for the offense itself. The anti-gangsterism offense, as it is sometimes called, was the one the Hells Angels feared most because if the entire East End chapter was deemed a criminal organization, the authorities could try to go after the club member's assets as proceeds of crime.

The province's then relatively new *Civil Forfeiture Act* places a reverse onus on the person seeking the return of seized assets to prove how they earned enough money to buy houses, property, jewelry and other "bling" as B.C.'s solicitor-general John Les once said while praising the new tool to fight crime.

John Virgil Punko, 39, a full-patch member of the East End chapter, was charged with conspiracy to produce and traffic methamphetamine, trafficking cocaine, two counts of possession of proceeds of crime, conspiracy to traffic cocaine, counseling mischief, conspiracy to commit extortion, conspiracy to commit mischief, conspiracy to commit assault, uttering threats, two counts of directing an offense in association with a criminal organization and four counts of commission of offense in association with a criminal organization.

Police alleged that between April 2004 and January 2005, Punko possessed almost $400,000 cash that constituted proceeds of crime, including $244,640 from methamphetamine distribution and $142,000 from the sale of five kilograms of cocaine.

Punko had a previous conviction from 2001 when he threatened Ernie Froess, a prosecutor in an earlier trial involving Hells Angels members Ronaldo Lising and Chico Pires. Punko was also charged in 1998 with extortion and possessing a prohibited weapon.

Randall Richard Potts, 45, another full-patch member of the East End chapter, was charged with conspiracy to traffic methamphetamine, conspiracy to produce methamphetamine, possession of proceeds of crime, possession of explosives, possession of explosives for a criminal organization, possession of a prohibited firearm, unauthorized possession of a firearm, two counts of extortion, uttering threats, two counts of trafficking in cocaine, two counts of directing an offense in association with a criminal organization and four counts of commission of offense in association with a criminal organization.

At the time, Potts had a lengthy criminal history that included charges of possession of a controlled substance, assault, possession of counterfeit money, mail theft, uttering threats and extortion. In all of these prior cases, with the exception of the assault charge, charges were stayed.

Potts was arrested in the parking lot of the North Burnaby Inn, located at 4125 Hastings Street in Burnaby, as he walked toward his black Hummer. He was wearing his Hells Angels colors. Room 133, the room he was living in at the hotel, was searched, as was another address in Surrey. At the Surrey location, the items seized were a Magner money counter and a handwritten list marked "Laboratory Items" that was found in a grey nylon bag in the closet. The document was later examined by a fingerprint expert, who found one print belonging to Potts on the back of the document and Potts' right thumb fingerprint on the front page.

Jean Joseph Violette, 54, a full-patch member of the East End chapter, was charged with extortion, conspiracy to commit extortion, possession of two illegal firearms and two counts of commission of offense in association with a criminal organization—"to wit, the East End Hells Angels." Violette had been previously convicted of assaulting a man in 2001.

Ronaldo Lising, 42, a full-patch member of the Nomads chapter of the Hells Angels, was charged with possession of methamphetamine for the purpose of trafficking, extortion and directing an offense in association with a criminal organization.

Lising was charged in 2005 with assault causing bodily harm after he allegedly punched and kicked a Burnaby man named Randall Bowles outside the Au Bar nightclub. Robert William Alvarez, another Vancouver member of the Hells Angels Nomads, was also accused in the incident. Lising was convicted in 2001 of trafficking cocaine with Hells Angels member Francisco Batista Pires, known as Chico, and sentenced to four and a half years in prison.

Richard Conway, 40, a full-patch member of the Vancouver chapter of the Hells Angels, was charged with conspiracy to traffic cocaine and trafficking cocaine.

Robert Leonard Thomas, 40, was a professional tattoo artist who operated the Kelowna shop Ritual Tattoo and a full-patch member of the East End chapter. After searching his Kelowna home, police charged Thomas with six weapons offenses, including possession of a prohibited weapon and possession of prohibited ammunition. He was convicted in 2004 of aggravated assault and assault causing bodily harm.

Jonathan Sal Bryce, 24, was the son of East End chapter president John Bryce. Bryce Jr. joined the Hells Angels but was a hangaround—he had not achieved full-member status at the time of his arrest. He was charged with four counts of trafficking cocaine, possession of the proceeds of crime, assault, conspiracy to commit extortion, extortion and two counts of the commission of an offense in association with a criminal organization.

Kerry Ryan Renaud, 25, was described by police as an associate of the East End chapter of the Hells Angels. He was charged with two counts of conspiracy to produce methamphetamine, trafficking methamphetamine and two counts of the commission of an offense in association with a criminal organization. Renaud had previously been arrested as a meth cook.

David Ronald Pearse, 27, an associate of the East End chapter, was charged with two counts of conspiracy to produce/traffic methamphetamine and two counts of committing an offense in association with a criminal organization. Pearse at the time had criminal convictions for the possession of a weapon for a dangerous purpose and possession of illegal drugs for the purpose of trafficking.

Nima Abbassian Ghavami, 25, an alleged associate of the East End chapter, was charged with two counts of conspiracy to produce/traffic methamphetamine, two counts of the commission of an offense in association with a criminal organization, and trafficking methamphetamine. Ghavami worked as a bouncer at the Cecil strip club in Vancouver, where he met Michael Plante. He had no previous criminal record.

Benjamin Azeroual, 26, was another associate of the East End chapter. He was charged with two counts of conspiracy to produce/traffic methamphetamine and two counts of the commission of an offense in association with a criminal organization.

Jason William Brown, 30, an associate of the East End chapter, was charged with two counts of conspiracy to produce/traffic methamphetamine and two counts of the commission of an offense in association with a criminal organization. Brown was sentenced to short jail terms after he was convicted in 1996 of the possession of narcotics for trafficking and in 1998 on a charge of impersonation. He also had convictions for driving while prohibited.

Wissam Mohamed Ayach, 26, an associate of the East End chapter, was charged with two counts of conspiracy to produce/traffic methamphetamine and two counts of commission of an offense in association with a criminal organization. Ayach had previously been convicted of possession of illegal drugs for the purpose of trafficking in 2002 and again in 2003.

Chad James Barroby, 27, an associate of the East End chapter, was charged with two counts of conspiracy to produce/traffic methamphetamine, two counts of trafficking cocaine and two counts of the commission of an offense in association with a criminal organization.

David Roger Revell, 41, an associate of the East End chapter, was charged with possession of cocaine for the purposes of trafficking, trafficking cocaine and the commission of an offense in association with a criminal organization.

Richard Andrew Rempel, 22, an associate of the East End chapter, was charged with possession of cocaine for the purpose of trafficking, trafficking cocaine and the commission of an offense in association with a criminal organization. In 2004, he had pleaded guilty to communicating for the purpose of prostitution in Kelowna.

Leroy Serra Pereira, 35, an associate of the East End chapter, was charged with conspiracy to commit mischief, conspiracy to commit extortion of Parminder Gill and the commission of an offense in association with a criminal organization.

Brian Jung, 35, an associate of the East End chapter, was charged with conspiracy to commit mischief, conspiracy to commit extortion and two counts of the commission of an offense in association with a criminal organization. These charges were later stayed.

· · ·

The E-Pandora bust came at a time when a number of incidents linked to the Hells Angels in Kelowna had attracted the attention of police, including a fight at Lake City Casino that was caught on a surveillance video. The video showed Hells Angels member Joe Calendino taking off his jacket to show his Hells Angels colors before punching a man at the casino.

Calendino, along with a Nomads chapter Hells Angel Jamie Holland, had been arrested in 2001 for weapons offenses after they were searched by police on Granville Mall. Calendino was caught carrying a loaded Kel Tec semiautomatic handgun and Holland had a loaded Combat Commander handgun with an altered serial number.*

---

* Calendino later became a drug addict and left the Hells Angels. He now lectures high school students about the evils of gang life.

Earlier in 2005, police had charged David Patrick O'Hara, a former member of the Vancouver chapter but at the time a Mission chapter member, with trafficking cocaine and the possession of a weapon. O'Hara pleaded guilty and was sentenced to just under three years for his crimes. He later left the Hells Angels and now works as a welding contractor.

Also busted in 2005 was Norman Edward Krogstad, then the 57-year-old president of the Hells Angels Vancouver chapter; he was charged with 14 counts of trafficking cocaine. He is the highest-ranking Hells Angels member to be convicted of drug trafficking in B.C.

Krogstad was among 10 men charged with trafficking cocaine and the possession of illegal guns; another was senior Vancouver chapter Hells Angels member Cedric Baxter Smith, then 55, of Langley. Krogstad and Smith pleaded guilty to 11 counts of trafficking nine kilograms of cocaine and were sentenced to four years in prison. They sold $400,000 worth of drugs to a police agent—an ex-member of the Prince George Renegades, an Angels puppet club—during a successful police operation code-named Project Essen.

The initial purchases were made after the police agent met Smith at his Langley home and at a nearby Wendy's restaurant—the police agent left the code 666 on Smith's pager as a signal to meet at the restaurant. The biker police agent also bought a kilogram of cocaine from Smith in Cache Creek and another kilo at the Canyon Alpine Motel in Boston Bar.

Smith went missing from his Langley home in May 2008 and is presumed dead.

Project Essen also resulted in charges against three members of the Prince George Renegades: Darrin Allan Massey, Derek Charles Timmins and George James McBeth, who pleaded guilty to the sale of firearms to a police agent in Prince George. Timmins sold a police agent an AK-47 assault rifle, 60 boxes (containing 1,200 rounds) of ammunition for the weapon and two semiautomatic pistols for $3,700. The serial numbers on all firearms were altered.

One Renegades member, William John Moore, the former president of the biker gang, was murdered shortly after he was charged in the Project Essen investigation. He was found in March 2005 shot to death in his car outside his Prince George house, which had been torched. His murder remains unsolved.

• • •

At the time the E-Pandora investigation began, the East End chapter comprised 19 members, and another six who were members of the elite Nomads chapter. The Nomads chapter has a clubhouse at 3910 Grant Street in an industrial area of Burnaby, a suburb of Vancouver.

Among some of the more prominent members of the chapter was John Peter Bryce, the president. He was the owner of a business called Hi-Way Choppers and part owner of a building, the Drake Hotel, which operated a popular strip club. Bryce was the sole director of a company that owned the hotel, which was sold for $3.2 million in 2007 to the City of Vancouver to meet the need for additional housing for the homeless in Vancouver's downtown Eastside.

Another member of the chapter was Michael Christiansen, known by the nickname Speedy. He moved to B.C. after he was acquitted in a Quebec court, along with three other Halifax Hells Angels, of the first-degree murders of five Quebec bikers.

Damiano Dipopolo was also a member of the East End chapter. At one time, he owned a hip-hop clothing store, Digstown Clothing, located on East Hastings in Burnaby. The store later moved to Kelowna. He appeared in three videos for the rap group

Swollen Members. In one video, Dipopolo wore a toque that said "Crime Inc." Dipopolo was a good friend of the lead singer, Mad Child, whose real name is Shane Bunting. Dipopolo and Bunting co-owned two houses in Kelowna. In a Swollen Members song, Mad Child raps: "Cops can suck my cock/If they don't like us to hang around prospects, strikers, bikers."

The singer complained in January 2011 that he was barred entry into the United States because of his association with the Hells Angels.

• • •

Before joining the Hells Angels Nomads in Vancouver, Ronaldo Lising was previously arrested for trafficking cocaine with Francisco (Chico) Pires. Both men were convicted in 2001 and sentenced to four and a half years in prison. It was the first significant prosecution of the Hells Angels in B.C. The key witness to testify against the bikers was an undercover civilian agent, Robert Molsberry, a former doorman at the No. 5 Orange club, who had been threatened over a drug debt before turning to police for help. He agreed to gather evidence against Lising and Pires in exchange for more than $25,000 and relocation under the witness protection program. Up to 45 officers targeted two Vancouver strip clubs as part of their investigation. Drug transactions took place outside the Hells Angels clubhouse in East Vancouver, gas stations, restaurants and gyms.

Former East End member Chico Pires, now a member of the Nomads chapter, was convicted with Lising of cocaine trafficking in 2001. At the time, Chico was the director of the company that owned a coffee bar, Big Shots Cafe, in the 3900-block of East Hastings in Burnaby. Chico's brother, George Batista Pires, also switched from the East End chapter to join the Nomads chapter.

One of the targets of E-Pandora was Lloyd (Louie) George Robinson, the half-brother of John Bryce. Robinson was once charged with the fatal beating of a Vancouver nightclub owner. The charge was later stayed. He was also charged in 1996 with extortion along with Hells Angels Nomads member Gino Zumpano, but that charge was also stayed. At one time Robinson was well-known for running a stripper agency. He left the Hells Angels after the E-Pandora charges were laid.

East End chapter member Joseph Bruce Skreptak was among those who bought a house in Kelowna. In May 2005, police busted a marijuana grow operation at a rural house owned by Skreptak on Highway 33 in the Kelowna area. Police seized 100 "mother" plants and about 1,000 "clones"—clippings started from high THC mother plants to produce starter plants for other grow-ops. A sign above the door leading to the room containing the mother plants said: "Support Your Local Hells Angels White Rock" to serve as a warning to anyone who might try to rip off the plants. Skreptak's truck, with a Hells Angels sticker on it, was parked at the home when police raided it. Skreptak wasn't charged, but the people renting the home were charged.

One of the most violent East End chapter members was Juel (Jules) Ross Stanton. In 2003, he was accused of taking part in the beating and robbery of John O'Shaughnessy to collect a debt, making the man sign over his Harley-Davidson and vintage GTO car as partial payment. The victim testified he thought police were going to bust a marijuana grow operation in a warehouse complex he rented space in, so he took the marijuana before police could get it. At trial, however, the judge found the victim had exaggerated his injuries and was a "manipulative liar." It didn't help that the victim, after he was relocated and paid $100,000 by police, was busted for operating another marijuana grow operation.

At one point when Stanton, whose nickname was Hooligan, was before the courts on two assault and extortion cases. A pickle jar marked "Juel Stanton Fund" was placed on top of the bar at the East End clubhouse to collect donations to help pay for Stanton's lawyers and to support his family.

One of the cases that Stanton was charged with involved a small-time marijuana grower named Alexander Goldman, who testified that he thought he was being busted by the cops one day in 2001 when a vehicle drove up carrying a group of men. Instead, Stanton got out wearing a Hells Angels T-shirt and told Goldman he and his buddies were taking over the grow-op. He told Goldman to get lost.

Goldman did as he was told, but later was contacted by a man who wanted to meet with him. He testified he was kidnapped and put in a van, and then beaten until both eyes were so swollen he could hardly see, and robbed of his wallet. He spent five days recovering in hospital with black eyes, fractured ribs and fractures to his facial bones.

At the time of his run-in with Stanton, Goldman was living under an assumed name in the witness protection program. He died of a stroke on October 28, 2004, before completing his testimony at the trial of Stanton and three other men—Stanton's brother Norman Clay Stanton, Jeffrey Michael Douglas and Damon Bartolomeo. They were accused but acquitted of kidnapping, beating, robbing and unlawfully confining Goldman. Juel Stanton was fatally gunned down in August 2010.

A fifth co-accused, Richard Doucet, also known as Frenchie, was under surveillance at the time for two murders that took place at a Surrey crack house. Doucet pleaded guilty to unlawfully confining Goldman and received a 23-month sentence and lifetime gun prohibition.

• • •

At the time of the E-Pandora bust, police estimated there were almost 100 Hells Angels members in B.C. According to a Criminal Intelligence Service Canada report, the Hells Angels are the largest outlaw motorcycle gang in Canada, with roughly 500 members in Canada. Canada has more Hells Angels per capita than any other country, including the United States, which has about 700 members in chapters in about 20 states. There are about 3,000 Hells Angels members worldwide.

For years, police in B.C. alleged that the Hells Angels were a criminal organization. The biker gang always countered that the Hells Angels was simply a bunch of guys who were motorcycle enthusiasts. The Hells Angels' media spokesman, Rick Ciarniello, suggested that while there may be a few bad apples within the Hells Angels, this was probably true of any organization, and a few bad apples don't make the entire club a criminal organization. Ciarniello has waged a public relations war with police for years. At times he seemed to be winning because there were never any serious charges laid against the bikers.

But the latest bust sent a message that the Hells Angels were no longer untouchable, and now police wanted the East End Hells Angels declared a criminal organization.

As police would soon find out, it wouldn't be easy to prove.

CHAPTER 8

The First E-Pandora Court Case

The E-Pandora investigation was a complex case, involving 19 co-accused and dozens of charges ranging from drug trafficking to extortion and weapons offenses. One massive trial was logistically impossible, because it would have dragged through the courts for years and raised the prospect that the accused would be acquitted because of delay.

The massive case resulted in five federal and two provincial indictments being filed. Trial dates were initially set for the next year, 2006, but were delayed by three pre-trial motions launched by the defense—challenges of the admissibility of the wiretap, the use of the police agent and a constitutional challenge of the criminal organization provisions of the Criminal Code, which the defense argued were overly broad.

The first case to proceed was the federal case against full-patch Hells Angels member Ronaldo (Ronnie) Lising and an alleged associate, Nima Ghavami. Lising was charged with the possession of methamphetamine for the purpose of trafficking with respect to one kilogram of the drug that he had directed Plante to take to Bob's Deli, which was owned by Lising's brother. Ghavami was charged with trafficking methamphetamine for his alleged role in the drug deal. He was ultimately acquitted of the charge.

The court case began with a pretrial abuse-of-process application filed in April 2006 but not heard until the following September. The application alleged police had abused their authority by allowing their police agent, Michael Plante, to commit crimes of drug trafficking and numerous assaults while he was infiltrating the Hells Angels.

Ghavami also filed a civil suit against the RCMP and Plante, alleging that the police agent had intimidated Ghavami into committing crimes. He stated that Plante had used force against him, and had even at one point stuck a gun into his mouth. Ghavami's lawyer, Don Morrison, a former prosecutor and B.C. police complaints commissioner, suggested that the police conduct was so "outrageous" that the courts should throw out the charges.

The civil suit was the first time the public learned that a civilian had penetrated the Hells Angels; it also publicly revealed the agent's name.

Similarly, Lising's lawyer, Greg DelBigio, argued that the public was endangered by the drug dealing and violence carried out by the police agent. DelBigio told B.C. Supreme Court Justice Victor Curtis, "The police were under a duty to ensure that the community was not endangered through Michael Plante's actions and yet the community was in danger," the lawyer argued. He further said the illegal actions of the agent violated his client's rights under Section 7 of Canada's Charter of Rights and Freedoms.

Third from the left is Francisco (Chico) Pires; East End president John Peter Bryce is sixth from the left; David Francis Giles, now a member of the Kelowna Hells Angels, is 10th from the left; Jule (Juels) Ross Stanton (deceased) is 12th from the left; 13th from the left is Jonathan Bryce, the son of the chapter president; Ronaldo Lising is on the far right, with sword in his left hand. This photo was seized by police during the 2005 clubhouse raid and was later entered as a court exhibit.

East End Hells Angels member Jean Joseph Violette. The photo was taken outside the Vancouver Law Courts during his trial, where he represented himself, so wore a suit and tie.

East End chapter president John Bryce surveys damage from the police raid on July 15, 2005.

Bryce shows damage to a door rammed by police during the same raid July 15, 2005.

East End Hells Angels member Damiano Dipopolo at his Digstown clothing store on East Hastings in Burnaby.

Hells Angels spokesman, Rick Ciarniello, at Vancouver chapter clubhouse.

Photo credit: Ian Smith/*Vancouver Sun*

Motorcycles parked outside the Hells Angels clubhouse in Coquitlam.

Photo credit: Ian Smith/*Vancouver Sun*

Rick Ciarniello at the door of the Coquitlam clubhouse.

Rick Cianarello, pictured above and below, in the Coquitlam clubhouse.

John Bryce

Hells Angels member Ronaldo (Ronnie) Lising.

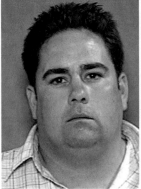

Vancouver Hells Angels member Glen Hehn.

Hells Angels member Francisco (Chico) Pires.

Hells Angels member David Francis Giles, aka the Gyrator.

Crystal meth cook Kerry Ryan Renaud.

East End Hells Angels member John Virgil Punko.

Ronaldo (Ronnie) Lising being arrested in 2000 for cocaine trafficking.

Juel (Jules) Ross Stanton from a police mug shot. He was gunned down in 2010.

Robert Thomas outside the East End clubhouse the day of the police raid July 15, 2005. He owns a tattoo shop in Kelowna.

A photo montage of B.C. Supreme Court Justice Peter Leask, whose face is superimposed over Bugs Bunny. This was posted on the Gangsters Out blog on Dec. 1, 2009 under the headline: Peter Leask Should Be Hanged for Treason (http://gangstersout.blogspot.com/2009/12/peter-leask-should-be-hanged-for.html). The blogger, whose identity remains a mystery, was reacting to Leask's ruling a few days earlier that the Crown could not proceed on criminal organization charges against Randy Potts and John Punko because a jury had earlier acquitted the pair on similar criminal organization charges.

Rick Ciarniello talks to the media (unidentified bikers in background) outside the Vancouver chapter clubhouse in 2002, after it was raided by the RCMP.

"How does authorizing the police to buy and sell drugs violate anyone's rights?" the judge asked the defense lawyer.

DelBigio suggested that the police tolerated Plante continuously acting outside the bounds of permissible activity, and, though police had the power to cancel Plante's contract, they chose not to.

The defense filed an RCMP document at the hearing that said Plante committed 58 illegal offenses while he was under the direction of his Mountie handlers. It mentioned Plante had a "know-it-all attitude" and could be difficult to work with.

During the 54-day hearing in the B.C. Supreme Court before Justice Victor Curtis, Plante was called to testify under heavy police protection—he was escorted in and out of court by plainclothes officers and taken out a side door so he would have no contact with the public. It was the first test of how Plante would stand up to grueling cross-examination by defense lawyers. Originally, he had been expected to testify only for a few days, but the cross-examination stretched into weeks and ultimately lasted for more than a month.

Plante testified that he committed illegal acts with the blessing of his police handlers. He said he would first discuss with police what he planned to do—at the direction of various Hells Angels members. The police preapproved the activity, and then monitored what was going on via various listening devices, including one installed in Plante's Mustang. Afterward, he explained, he would meet with his handlers, often showing them the illegal drugs and cash, which the police photographed. The items were then either seized by police or used to complete the planned drug transaction.

He admitted he was paid up to $14,000 a month by the RCMP, plus expenses, which he spent on things like expensive dinners to impress his Angels buddies to show how well he was doing in the drug trade. One night, he recalled, he went out for dinner with Hells Angels Chico Pires, Rob Alvarez and Damiano Dipopolo, and on to the Cecil for drinks, ending the evening in the Au Bar nightclub. Plante said he picked up the $2,000 tab for the evening. He said he paid cash, even though this made it difficult to be reimbursed by police because they needed receipts; receipts, however, were suspicious because the Angels knew he didn't have a bank account.

"It looked very, very strange asking for a receipt," Plante testified. "Most of the Angels knew I didn't have a bank account." He also bought tickets for B.C. Lions football games and once paid $800 for Hells Angels members to attend a Vancouver performance by comedian Jerry Seinfeld, but no one wanted to go to the show.

"Did police ever question the rate you were spending money?" DelBigio asked Plante. Never, the witness replied. But he admitted it was very stressful having police monitoring him all the time. A recording was played in court where Plante was questioned by one of his handlers, inspector Gary Shinkaruk, who asked Plante about his companions at a sushi restaurant one particular evening.

"Are you watching me 24/7?" Plante asked on the tape, sounding annoyed. Shinkaruk explained that a police surveillance team was watching a number of targets who sometimes crossed paths with Plante.

"It added to my stress, big time," Plante testified about having very little private life at the time.

Plante testified he was aware that his police agent contract could be terminated if he committed a crime of violence or a drug offense that had not been sanctioned by police in advance. But sometimes this was difficult, he said. At the time, he was working as a bouncer at the Cecil Hotel strip club and would sometimes be involved in three fights a night. He couldn't phone police every time a fight broke out in the bar. He recalled one particular night having to slap Ghavami, then a bouncer at the Cecil, to prevent him from driving home drunk from work.

"I told him he was too drunk to drive home," Plante recalled, adding he took away Ghavami's helmet so he couldn't ride his rented Harley-Davidson. "He kept coming at me aggressively," Plante recalled. "I said 'Go away.' I slapped him and he went down." Ghavami's girlfriend later came to pick him up, he said.

Plante was questioned about his use of steroids, which body builders use to "bulk up" their muscle mass. Steroids are also known to have a side effect that affects a person's temper, often referred to as "roid rage." Plante admitted he was a steroid user who, at the time, was heavily involved in weightlifting; he weighed 240 pounds (109 kilograms) and was able to bench-press 400 pounds (180 kilos). But he denied that steroids made him a hothead, pointing out he only used half a tablet a day.

Police involved in Project E-Pandora also testified at the hearing, explaining it was necessary for Plante to commit drug crimes and assaults or it would have drawn the suspicion of the Hells Angels, thereby putting Plante's safety in jeopardy.

Drug cases in Canada are the sole jurisdiction of the federal government, which assigned veteran prosecutor Martha Devlin to the case. She was tough and vigorously defended what she believed was the fine work carried out by police in the investigation. At times, she became indignant at defense attacks on the integrity of not only police but the Crown as well.

Devlin told the judge that any illegal activities undertaken by Michael Plante were exempt under Section 25.1 of the Criminal Code, which permits the commission of acts that would otherwise constitute offenses, without prior, independent judicial authorization.

Devlin conceded that while Plante may have been egotistical and occasionally confrontational with his police handlers, he was never out of control, nor was he a danger to the public. He definitely wasn't running amok, she said.

"Michael Plante was committing acts at the direction of members of the Hells Angels, specifically the East End chapter of the Hells Angels. What we see from the investigation conducted by the RCMP is that it's not the RCMP who consider themselves above the law, but members of the East End chapter of the Hells Angels who consider themselves above the law." She then added, "While there may have been isolated instances of illegality, the police did not plan or cause these events. They simply reacted to them in a way that minimized the risks involved."

The Crown admitted that if the defense was successful in its abuse-of-process application, the charges would have to be dropped against Lising and Ghavami. They also admitted that the ability of law-enforcement agents to investigate organized crimes would be seriously hampered.

On March 16, 2007, the judge ruled in the Crown's favor, finding that while the police agent did take part in illegal activity, his actions met the test to be exempt under the law. The police and prosecutors, while confident the judge would not find any police misconduct, nevertheless breathed a sigh of relief to have the court confirm this.

Outside the court, Gary Shinkaruk said he was "very pleased" by the ruling. "There certainly was a concern which way it would go, so I am very satisfied," he told reporters. "I look forward to moving on to the prosecution phase now and bringing the evidence yet again before the courts so the judge can make the decision on E-Pandora." He also confirmed that the RCMP investigation had cost more than $10 million to date.

• • •

Defense lawyer Don Morrison, however, suggested the RCMP's behavior verged on criminal negligence by allowing the police agent to distribute dozens of kilograms of crystal methamphetamine into Surrey during the E-Pandora operation.

"It is not the kind of national police force that I want in Canada, when they allow 60 pounds of methamphetamine to go into the Surrey community with no warnings whatsoever to the citizens," the lawyer told *Vancouver Sun* reporter Kim Bolan outside court. He suggested that the police allowing the deadly drug to be sold on the street would increase addiction and could have caused fatal drug overdoses.

"How can you have a police force that kills our citizens?" Morrison asked reporters. Morrison showed them a copy of a letter he had written to Attorney General Wally Oppal and Surrey mayor Diane Watts, urging the appointment of a special prosecutor to investigate the RCMP's conduct.

"Large-scale criminal conduct such as is evident in Project E-Pandora undermines the whole criminal justice system," Morrison's letter said. "I trust you will see fit to investigate this matter and ensure that in future, the citizens of our province are protected by the police, and are not the victims of their criminal activity."

Morrison reminded reporters that 44 people in B.C. had died from crystal meth overdoses in 2004. "They were aiding and abetting the trafficking of crystal meth," Morrison said. "It makes no sense to me that this conduct should be condoned."

At the time, Ghavami was standing beside his lawyer and was asked by Kim Bolan three times if he was against trafficking crystal meth. "I guess so, yes," the accused meth trafficker finally admitted.

• • •

The case was scheduled to proceed to trial 10 days later on March 26, 2007. On the first day of the trial, Lising's lawyers, Greg DelBigio and Jason Gratl, filed a constitutional challenge of section 25.1 of the Criminal Code and its regulations, arguing that Lising's rights guaranteed by Section 7 of the Canadian Charter of Rights and Freedoms had been violated. The defense argued that the law should be found unlawful and struck down.

Justice Curtis, however, ordered that the trial should proceed and that the constitutional challenge be heard after the trial, if it proved necessary.

Following a 12-day trial, on April 18 the judge ruled that the Crown had proven the charges against Lising beyond a reasonable doubt, but no finding of guilt was entered, pending the hearing of the constitutional challenge. At the same time, Ghavami was acquitted.

The trial heard how Plante's methamphetamine supplier had at one point delivered a package of methamphetamine to Ghavami's apartment, although Plante had not asked him to. The judge, however, found no evidence indicating that Ghavami knew what was in the package. A wiretap heard Ghavami telling Plante he had repackaged the substance for him, though he did not refer to it as methamphetamine.

"In my opinion, it is reasonably possible in such circumstances that Mr. Ghavami believed the substance to be something other than a controlled substance," Justice Curtis concluded. "He could, for instance, have repackaged it because it was a dry powder in a plastic bag, was liable to break and spill, rather than because he was trying to hide its identity."

The judge pointed out that Plante had testified that Ghavami was not involved in criminal activity at the time and he didn't want him involved because he was a friend. Plante testified that he thought that the police had "tunnel vision" and that officers wouldn't listen to him about Ghavami. "I tried to keep him out of it," Plante recalled.

"There is no evidence that Mr. Ghavami profited in any way from receiving the package and giving it to Michael Plante," Justice Curtis said. Ghavami's lawyer, Don Morrison, was pleased with the ruling. The Crown did not appeal the acquittal of Ghavami, who was still to face another trial.

• • •

Lising's constitutional challenge was heard during a two-day hearing in May, when the defense argued that the law allowing the actions of police agent Michael Plante should be found unconstitutional. On June 22, 2007, Justice Curtis dismissed the defense application.

"In this case, Michael Plante, the police agent, was required to be available to perform services for the East End Chapter of the Hells Angels at all times of the day or night," the judge found. "Not being able to take part in criminal activity on very short notice could easily jeopardize an undercover operation. While the result of failing to apprehend a child in need of apprehension is more immediately obvious, the loss of a police agent's successful connection with criminal targets could well result in ensuing social damage of equal or greater gravity."

The judge went on to say that the ultimate goal of Parliament in enacting section 25.1 of the Criminal Code was the protection of everyone's right to "life, liberty and security of the person. Neither the provisions of section 25.1 of the Criminal Code, nor those of the *Controlled Drugs and Substances Act (Police Enforcement) Regulations*, are contrary to Section 7 of the Charter. The claim for remedy . . . is dismissed," the judge concluded.

Lising was convicted and sentenced to four and a half years in prison. He began serving his sentence immediately, although he was still facing another trial on weapons and extortion charges, which did not commence for another year.

In the meantime, Jonathan Sal Bryce, the son of John Bryce, the president of the East End chapter of the Hells Angels, pleaded guilty to four counts of trafficking in cocaine, totaling five kilos, possession of the proceeds of crime and the extortion of Glen Louie. He was sentenced to six years in prison.

Federal prosecutor Martha Devlin had urged the judge to send Bryce to jail for eight years, describing him as a "professional drug trafficker" and a low-ranking member of the Hells Angels motorcycle gang. The sentencing judge, B.C. Supreme Court associate chief justice Patrick Dohm, said he would have sent 26-year-old Bryce to prison for up to 10 years had it not been for his relatively young age, his expression of remorse in a letter to the court and the fact that this was his first offense.

The judge admitted that after watching a surveillance video during the sentencing hearing and listening to wiretap phone calls played in court by the prosecution, he found Bryce's handling of himself during drug deals was "at a comfort level that absolutely scares me." Bryce seemed to have access to unlimited quantities of cocaine, the judge added. Bryce sold one kilogram to Plante on three occasions, including two sales inside the Hells Angels clubhouse, and another deal involving two kilograms.

The judge said he hoped Bryce could turn his life around after he paid his debt to society by serving his prison sentence.

At the time of the offenses, Bryce was an official friend of the Hells Angels chapter and was promoted to hangaround status a day after taking part in the beating on January 21, 2005, of drug dealer Glen Louie with Hells Angels member Jean Violette. Louie was beaten because he was holding himself out to be a Hells Angels associate in order to sell drugs on the North Vancouver First Nations reserve. A tape-recording of the beating, in which the victim could be heard moaning, was played in court. Bryce received a three-year sentence, to be served concurrently with his drug sentence, for his role in the extortion.

Defense lawyer Ken Westlake told the judge that his client grew up in North Vancouver, where he worked at the Lynn Valley Safeway for three years before graduating from high school as an honor student. He later took an electronics course at BCIT and then worked for a firm installing surveillance systems.

"Full-time drug dealers do not usually have jobs," the lawyer told the court, adding his client bought a house and opened a tanning salon, which he was running when he was arrested. "This is a young man who seriously regrets the pain he has caused, particularly to his grandparents, and the stress it caused his family," Westlake said. Bryce's father was in court for the sentencing and watched his son be led away to begin serving prison time.

The judge granted a defense request to recommend to prison authorities that Jonathan Bryce serve his time at Ferndale, a minimum-security prison in the Fraser Valley. This would allow the young man to continue having visits and the support of his family and friends. Ferndale was known as Club Fed, because of its waist-high fences, and the fact that it once had a golf course, which was shut down after the Reform Party prompted a public outcry about it.

Jonathan Bryce's guilty plea caused conflict among East End Hells Angels members because it came without notice and made things more difficult for those still facing trial. At one point, Bryce tried to withdraw his guilty plea, then changed his mind again and let it stand.

• • •

The next trial, involving Hells Angels senior member David Francis Giles and two co-accused Kelowna men, would prove to be an important test for the police and prosecutors. It was the first case in B.C. involving an allegation that the East End Hells Angels was a criminal organization.

For years police in B.C. had alleged that the Hells Angels was a criminal organization and was the number one criminal threat in B.C. Specifically, police said the Hells Angels East End chapter was one of the richest and most powerful Hells Angels chapters in Canada. The Hells Angels, however, repeatedly refuted the claim, calling it "police propaganda" and a "smear campaign" aimed at boosting police budgets to increase the number of officers to combat bikers and organized crime.

Rick Ciarniello, a senior Hells Angels member who acted as media spokesperson for the organization, often explained that there might be a few Angels with criminal records, but that didn't make the entire motorcycle club a criminal organization, saying that if a few Vancouver cops were charged with criminal offenses, it didn't mean the entire police force was a criminal organization.

"If I was going to be a criminal, if that is what I wanted to be, the last thing I would do is want to wear a sign on my back and to ride the kind of motorcycle that I do. It makes no sense," Ciarniello told reporter Kim Bolan in 2004. Asked why the Hells

Angels clubhouses are so heavily fortified, Ciarniello replied that it was to keep people from breaking in and stealing things. He added that sometimes "loons"come to the Hells Angels and ask them to kill people and collect debts.

Responding to comments made by then-Vancouver police chief Jamie Graham calling on the public to rid the city of the "scourge" of outlaw bikers in Canada, Ciarniello told reporters, "If they [police] had real evidence we were involved in the things they allege, they wouldn't have to be making these statements—they'd go out and bust people."

"There have been no criminal convictions under gang legislation out here," Ciarniello added. He was referring to a landmark case in 2005 when an Ontario Superior Court judge found that two men, Ray Bonner and Steven (Tiger) Lindsay, had committed extortion in association with the Hells Angels.

"I am satisfied beyond a reasonable doubt that during the time period specified in count two of the indictment, the Hells Angels Motorcycle Club as it existed in Canada was a criminal organization," Justice Michelle Fuerst concluded in the Lindsay and Bonner case, which involved the $75,000 extortion of a person from Barrie, Ontario.

At the time of the extortion, Lindsay and Bonner wore clothing bearing the insignia of the East End Hells Angels. Justice Fuerst concluded that the two men were dressed that way in order to use the Hells Angels reputation for extreme violence to aid their extortion.

The judge also referred to Ciarniello in the judgment, citing the minutes of a B.C. Hells Angels officers' meeting where Ciarniello and two other men met with a man identified as a Quebec Hells Angel in negotiations to try to end the war between the Hells Angels and the Rock Machine. The Ontario judgment also noted the fact that a wiretap of a Hells Angels member overheard the Quebec biker saying that former Montreal member David Giles was now living in British Columbia.

In an earlier court ruling in 2005, B.C. Supreme Court justice Ross Lander commented that "it is a notorious fact that the Hells Angels are involved in organized crime, and that such crime crosses provincial and national borders is generally known and accepted, and a fact of which judicial notice may be taken."

However, the conclusions of Justice Lander in B.C. and Justice Fuerst in Ontario could have no bearing on future cases. Each case brought under Canada's anti-gang law—sections 467.1(1) to 467.2(2) of the Criminal Code, which makes it illegal to commit crime as a member of or in association with a criminal organization defined as three or more people acting together for a common purpose—has to be proved on its own merits every time a "gangsterism" charge is brought before a superior court in Canada.

Until 2005, with the charges laid as a result of the Project E-Pandora investigation, police had never tried to have a B.C. court declare the Hells Angels a criminal organization. The road ahead would prove to be a long one, with many detours.

At the outset of the trial, Rick Ciarniello filed a constitutional challenge of the anti-gang law in the B.C. Supreme Court, arguing that his Charter rights had been violated by Justice Fuerst's ruling in Ontario. To back his claim, Ciarniello filed an affidavit saying his freedom to speak to the media to advocate on behalf of the Hells Angels had been severely limited because of the Ontario ruling. He claimed that after the Ontario ruling, he had been subjected to harassment by law-enforcement officials, ostracism in the community, and continued to suffer "the stigma associated with being a member of a club that has now been declared a criminal organization."

The ruling made him more guarded about speaking with the press "because of my concern that I may be charged with participating in the activities of a criminal organization, an offence under section 476.11 of the Criminal Code," Ciarniello's affidavit said. He said the effect of the Ontario ruling "is to declare me a member of a criminal organization notwithstanding that I have never engaged in the promotion of criminal conduct." Ciarniello, who at the time was 61, noted in his affidavit that he was a law-abiding Hells Angels member who was "not responsible for the criminal acts that have, at times, been committed by some of its members."

He gave specific examples of how people had treated him differently after the Ontario ruling: he recalled going one night to a Joey Tomatoes restaurant in Coquitlam, where he overheard a couple asking to be moved because "they did not want to sit next to a criminal, namely a member of the Hells Angels." This made him uncomfortable, so he decided to leave the restaurant, he said.

"I have noticed a marked difference in the way that people respond to me when I am wearing my colors," Ciarniello stated in his affidavit. "The mood has gone from friendly and casual curiosity to fear, loathing and avoidance such that I am made to feel uncomfortable wearing the HAMC [Hells Angels Motorcycle Club] insignia."

He said staff members at the local Safeway near his Port Coquitlam home, where he has purchased groceries for 20 years, were not as friendly as they used to be, and he received similar treatment at a Shell gas station. His affidavit also claimed that, after the Ontario ruling, John Bryce Sr. was refused service as a customer of the Bank of Nova Scotia after two decades of doing business there.

B.C. Supreme Court justice Bill Ehrcke dismissed Ciarniello's constitutional challenge. The judge found that even if Ciarniello could prove the facts in his petition, it must be dismissed because Ciarniello "does not have public interest standing to bring his petition," so could not prove his Charter rights were infringed.

• • •

It also didn't help the Hells Angels public relations campaign that one of its members, Villy Roy Lynnerup of the White Rock chapter, was caught carrying a loaded gun when he went through airport security screening at Vancouver International Airport en route to catching a plane to Edmonton in April 2006.

The loaded Bryco .38-caliber semiautomatic pistol was in a black canvas carry-on bag, which went through an X-ray machine while Lynnerup walked through the metal detector. Also found among Lynnerup's possessions was "substantial information" related to club and national Hells Angels activities, as well as Hells Angels T-shirts and a vest displaying club "colors" indicating Lynnerup was the sergeant at arms for his chapter.

Lynnerup was charged with possession of an unlicensed, unregistered firearm, possessing a loaded prohibited firearm and carrying a concealed weapon. At trial, he stated that the gun was not his and that he didn't know how it came to be in his bag. He also argued that no one would be so stupid as to think they could escape detection through airport security scanners. A provincial court judge convicted him on all three counts, sentencing him to 18 months and imposing a lifetime firearms ban.

"I'm absolutely flabbergasted that this has happened," Ciarniello told *Vancouver Sun* reporter Darah Hansen just after Lynnerup's arrest. "This is so absurd it almost sounds like a setup. I can't believe anybody would try to do something like that."

CHAPTER 9

Criminal Organization, Round One

The first Hells Angels criminal organization test case in B.C. involved a man police had been interested in for some time: David Francis Giles, who was a former Sherbrooke Hells Angels chapter member before moving to B.C. to join the East End chapter.

When Giles was busted in 2005, he had been living the good life in Kelowna, where he was trying to establish a new Hells Angels chapter. He had a large house on the side of a mountain, where he liked to hike among the Ponderosa pines, bunch grass and sage that dotted the hillside.

Giles, who called himself Gyrator, was accused of a trafficking conspiracy charge involving an eight-kilogram cocaine seizure. Two other Kelowna-area residents, David Roger Revell, known as Baldy because of his shaved head, and his underling, Richard Andrew Rempel, were also busted.

Revell and Rempel faced counts of trafficking cocaine and possession for the purpose of trafficking cocaine. The trio were also charged with possession of cocaine for the purpose of trafficking for the benefit of, at the direction of, or in association with a criminal organization, to wit: the East End Chapter of the Hells Angels. Revell and Rempel were also charged with trafficking cocaine. It is sometimes referred to as a gangsterism charge because it makes it illegal for gangsters to commit crimes in association with a criminal organization, which is defined as at least three people.

The Giles trial began with a pretrial legal challenge of the judge's authorization of the wiretap that allowed police to secretly record the conversations of Giles and Revell. Giles' lawyer, Richard Fowler, and Revell's lawyer, Doug Jevning, argued that the authorization was invalid because the interception of the two men's private communications violated their section 8 rights under the Charter of Rights and Freedoms, so the conversations should be ruled inadmissible.

The lawyers argued that the wiretap authorization was based on errors made in the supporting affidavit, which alleged that there were reasonable and probable grounds to believe Giles was committing or had committed extortion involving UN gang leader Clay Roueche, and was involved in a conspiracy to commit assault with a weapon or assault causing bodily harm with other members of the East End Hells Angels to avenge the assault on Michael Plante at Brandi's nightclub on October 15, 2004.

Defense counsel pointed out that no evidence was gathered against Giles during the wiretap to support the police allegations, so Plante must be considered an unreliable source. The defense also argued that Plante was motivated to fabricate information because of the huge payments being made to him by police pointing to payments between December 10, 2004, and January 8,

2005, totaling $201,232.47, comprising $10,000 to Plante himself, $29,232.45 for expenses and $162,000 to purchase drugs.

While the defense lawyers did not suggest that the payments to Plante amounted to abuse, they said Plante wanted them to continue because he must have been living a "pretty good life" as the expenses paid included trips and car leases.

"I observe, however, that the authorizing judge read all about the payments to Plante," Associate Chief Justice Anne MacKenzie noted in her June 22, 2007, ruling, dismissing the defense application. "I do not find the affiant's error to be fatal, either in isolation or combined with any of the other errors relied upon by defense counsel. They were all minor. None was an attempt to bolster Plante's reliability. I infer they were inadvertent mistakes."

There were two similar wiretap challenges made by the defense, but the judge upheld as valid all three wiretap authorizations involving Giles, which allowed police to intercept his private communications from January 12 through to July 28, 2005.

The defense also challenged the admissibility of wiretap conversations Plante had with Randy Potts, John Punko, Ronaldo Lising, Lloyd Robinson and Tom Gillis to prove the East End Hells Angels was a criminal organization.

The Crown subpoenaed Punko, Potts and Lising to testify at the Giles trial. They all refused and were cited for contempt of court. The judge put off their sentencing until the Giles trial was finished. Another East End Hells Angels member, Jean Violette, was also called to testify. He cooperated and adopted statements he made to Plante, so they were not considered hearsay.

During the hearing, the defense conceded that the statements of Potts, Punko and Lising were admissible under "the exception to the hearsay rule because the criteria of necessity and reliability are met." The judge ruled those statements were admissible.

But the defense disputed the admissibility of the statements of Gillis and Robinson, arguing they constituted hearsay evidence and did not fall within any exception to the hearsay rule. The judge ruled that the statements of Robinson and Gillis were not admissible to prove the truth of their content, but for the limited purpose of "showing the state of mind of the declarant, or their effect on the listener, if relevant."

The defense also challenged allowing as an expert witness inspector Andy Richards, who was with the Organized Crime Agency of B.C. at the time of the investigation, but was at the time of the trial in charge of operations at the Port Moody police department. The court was told that Richards had spent 17 of his 25 years as a police officer investigating the activities of the Hells Angels, and in particular the activities of the East End Hells Angels, and had special knowledge about other chapters of the Hells Angels in B.C.

The defense argued that the court should not allow Richards to give expert testimony about the main purposes and activities of the East End Hells Angels because that evidence was not necessary. The defense argued that his evidence "is more compelling than reliable, and ought to be excluded on that basis."

"I disagree," Justice MacKenzie concluded on January 17, 2008. "There is utterly no danger of this trier of fact being mesmerized or unduly influenced by any mystique surrounding the opinion of an experienced police officer."

Just as the trial was getting ready to start, on January 22, 2008, Justice MacKenzie imposed a sweeping ban on publication of the entire proceedings. The ban was imposed to protect the right to a fair trial of the co-accused in other E-Pandora trials, which were also in the midst of hearing pretrial applications.

But after an application by media lawyer Dan Burnett, representing the *Vancouver Sun*, the *Province* and Global TV, the judge varied the ban to allow some reporting of the trial, but not the names of accused still facing trial. The publication ban would make things a legal minefield for the media in the coming months, as other bans were put in place by other trial judges, but at least the public would learn some details of what took place in Kelowna.

Once the Giles trial began hearing evidence, it appeared to be a slam dunk for the Crown as far as the two co-accused Revell and Rempel were concerned. The Crown led evidence about the three kilograms of cocaine seized from the storage locker, which Rempel was observed entering via surveillance. There was also evidence about the sale of a kilo of cocaine to a drug dealer who was caught red-handed running from the cops with the coke in a bag. Finally, evidence was adduced about the efforts of Revell and Rempel to get rid of the Intrepid, which had a secret compartment containing another five kilos of cocaine, along with the surveillance tying both men to their not-so-cryptic BlackBerry messages.

The real challenge was trying to tie Giles to the drugs. There was no physical evidence against him, only some conversations with Revell, which the defense argued were vague and open to interpretation. "The Crown has presented no evidence of what Giles actually did," Giles' lawyer, Richard Fowler, said in his final argument to the judge. "What cogent evidence is there that he's engaged in criminal activity?"

Fowler admitted that Giles didn't like talking on the phone, but preferred to meet Revell in person. "In some circumstances, this might be suspicious, but in this case it is clear that Giles simply has a general aversion to talking on the phone because he no doubt believes that all his phones are being tapped," he said.

"Because someone chooses to guard their privacy does not lead to the inference that it is because they must be engaged in criminal activity. As a society, we jealously guard the right to privacy—that is why prior judicial authorization is required before an interception can take place," the lawyer added. "How many people would be prepared to talk freely on the phone believing that the state was intercepting all their communications?"

Fowler went on to discuss the conversation between Giles and his common-law partner, when she asked about charging airfares to Calgary for David Revell on her credit card. In response, Giles said Revell "made me thirty grand in the last few months," which the Crown alleged was money from cocaine trafficking.

"It is impossible to say with any certainty how Revell made Giles thirty grand," the defense lawyer argued. Revell might have given Giles a stock tip, he added. "It would be the purest of speculation to make any suggestion on how Revell was going to make Giles money or how much, or whether it was going to be a legitimate business transaction or an illegal venture of some kind."

After a 10-month trial, the prosecution offered no evidence to prove Giles ever possessed or controlled the nine kilograms of cocaine seized by police in Kelowna in 2005, the defense lawyer said. "In this case, there's no evidence of who supplied the cocaine. There is no evidence that he paid for the cocaine," he added.

Fowler suggested the Crown had taken evidence and molded it to fit its theory that Giles was involved in a "joint venture" with two co-accused in possessing the cocaine for the purposes of trafficking. He cited the conversation in Giles' home on May 2, 2005, when the biker was heard discussing the seized cocaine and telling Revell: "We'll get back up," which the Crown argued was clear evidence indicating both Revell and Giles were involved with the seized cocaine along with further discussion about how much money they owed for the drugs. Fowler argued, however, that the quality of the recording was so poor that the words attributed to Giles were not clear.

Fowler also reviewed a number of phone calls to show Giles was not directing or controlling Revell and Rempel. The three men were simply friends who often discussed things over the phone and in person, he said.

Police surveillance observed Giles and Revell meeting outside a Kelowna gym called Reflex—the eight-minute meeting occurred as police were seizing the car containing the five kilograms of cocaine. But what might have been discussed at that meeting is simply speculation, Fowler said, cautioning the judge about making inferences not based on foundations of fact.

The lawyer pointed out that during a wiretap conversation between Giles and Revell on May 2, 2005, they discussed the loss of eight kilograms of cocaine, which indicated only that Giles had knowledge of the cocaine, but was not controlling or directing Revell or the drugs.

"You have to be extremely careful about relying on after-the-fact conversations to infer knowledge," Fowler told the judge.

The judge pointed out that Giles was heard saying in the Kelowna clubhouse: "I deal in drugs." But Fowler said the comment must be viewed in its context—that Giles was discussing what police believed at the time. "He's relaying what he's been told [by police]," the defense lawyer suggested.

Fowler pointed out that Giles knew he was under police surveillance and was overheard by police saying in the Kelowna clubhouse: "I just don't pay attention to 'em, I don't give a fuck because where am I going? A hardware store or somewhere... I don't care. I don't try to lose them or anything."

Federal prosecutor Martha Devlin argued that several calls involving Giles proved that the men were working together trafficking cocaine in association with the notorious Hells Angels Motorcycle Club. She cited the conversation where Giles discussed with his partner how Revell had made $30,000 for him over the past several months.

"That all simply demonstrates that Revell and Giles are indeed in business," the prosecutor said. "That establishes that there's a joint venture . . . and that there is an association between the two of them."

Devlin said Giles, a 20-year member of the club, was the "quintessential" Hells Angel, and there is not a citizen he meets who he doesn't make sure knows who they're dealing with, she said. "He's got the jewelry, the clothing, all the paraphernalia at this house, the plaques and the stickers."

Citing the call in which Giles tells Revell, "We'll get back up" after the cocaine seizure, Devlin argued it was proof that all three men were involved in the joint venture, which went toward aiding the bid to expand the East End chapter into Kelowna.

"Giles is in control," Devlin argued about the dynamics of the conversation. "Giles is not deterred by the fact the cocaine has been seized and they must pay back the money."

• • •

Before the judge delivered her verdict, Hells Angels member Jean Violette made an application to continue the ban on publication of his name and other Hells Angels members still facing trial.

"I'm not an attorney, so it's hard for me to quote any precedents of law, so I'd like to speak, I guess, from the bottom of my gut, is what I'm trying to say," the biker, dressed in a suit and tie, told the judge. He was representing himself in court, as he would at trial.

"Lifting this ban would be prejudicial to myself and would interfere with my right to a fair trial," Violette continued. "We're not going to be given a fair chance to be tried for our crimes," the biker said. "Alleged crimes," he quickly added.

Violette, who said he was up all night doing research on the Internet in preparation for the hearing to consider extending the ban, said media stories often contain sensational and inflammatory information, which was the basis for his objection to the ban being lifted. The biker cited an "insatiable appetite the media has about the Hells Angels, and anything and everything that has to do with our motorcycle club."

Violette suggested if the judge ruled in the Giles case that the East End Hells Angels was a criminal organization, there would be a "media frenzy" once the ban was lifted. "The headlines of such a ruling will be splattered across the front pages of newspapers and will be broadcast over and over again on television stations," the biker argued.

A half dozen defense lawyers representing Hells Angels and alleged associates also opposed the application to lift the publication ban on the evidence of two expert witnesses who testified in detail about the outlaw motorcycle gang at Giles' trial.

The judge reserved her decision on the media application. She later decided to continue the ban on the names of the Hells Angels still facing trial and the evidence of the expert police witnesses who testified about the Hells Angels in B.C. and their relationship with other chapters worldwide.

• • •

On March 27, 2008, the judge rendered her verdict in the Giles trial. It was a crushing blow to the police and prosecutors. While the judge found Revell and Rempel guilty of trafficking cocaine, she acquitted Giles. "I have considered all of the evidence in its totality, and it does not prove beyond a reasonable doubt that Giles had a measure of control over the cocaine," Justice MacKenzie concluded. She found the Crown's interpretation of the evidence "strained" and "weak," finding the intercepted discussions the Crown contended related to the offense "unreliable."

"The Crown has over-interpreted Giles' statements and used the expert evidence to see an agenda that has no basis in the evidence," the judge said in a lengthy written ruling.

"The totality of the evidence fails to prove the guilt of Giles beyond a reasonable doubt. Cumulatively considered, the gaps in the evidence are fatal to the Crown's case. They cannot be filled by speculation, or 'shrewd guesses.' I agree with counsel for Giles that the evidence against Giles is sparse, and no amount of context or theory fitting can fill the gaps in the Crown's case," MacKenzie concluded.

She went on to say that "whatever knowledge Giles had after Revell and Rempel committed the offense is insufficient to prove he had knowledge and control, and therefore possession, of the cocaine at the time the offense was committed."

And the final blow to the Crown's case: "Because Giles is not guilty of the predicate offense, count two [the criminal organization charge] fails as against all the accused. It is therefore unnecessary to consider or address all the evidence called on whether the East End Hells Angels is a criminal organization, including the expert evidence on the nature, activities, and purposes of the Hells Angels, the agent's evidence, and the intercepted private communications."

A number of Hells Angels who were in court for the ruling—including Jean Violette—shook Giles' hand and congratulated him. Giles left the courtroom grinning. The police looked grim.

"I'm upset and I'm disappointed," then-Chief Superintendent Bob Paulson, the RCMP officer who had been in charge of the

E-Pandora operation, said after the verdict. At the time of the trial, Paulson was in charge of national security, criminal operations, in Ottawa.

Paulson, now an RCMP deputy commissioner, said Giles, who was 58 at the time he was acquitted, "was a very high priority for us." He added that Giles remained a suspect in the 2001 seizure of a 2.8 ton shipment of cocaine headed to B.C. aboard a vessel named the *Western Wind*, which was intercepted by authorities in Washington State.

"Mr. Giles can now get back to work in Kelowna," Paulson said sarcastically. "We're not done yet. We still have two more significant trials." He remained hopeful that the East End Hells Angels would be declared a criminal organization at the upcoming trials.

CHAPTER 10

Criminal Organization, Round Two

Police were hoping the next trial, involving two full-patch Hells Angels members and nine associates accused of being involved in producing and distributing crystal meth, would lead to a landmark ruling that would declare the East End Hells Angels a criminal organization.

John Virgil Punko and Randy Potts were charged by direct indictment on seven counts, including conspiracy to produce and traffic methamphetamine for the benefit of, at the direction of, or in association with a criminal organization, the East End chapter of the Hells Angels. The co-conspirators in the scheme were Hells Angels associates Kerry Ryan Renaud, the meth cook; his partner in the cook, David Ronald Pearse; Wissam Mohamed Ayach; Nima Ghavami; Jason William Brown; Chad James Barroby; and Benjamin Azeroual.

Supreme Court Justice Harvey Groberman was assigned as the trial judge, but when he was elevated to the B.C. Court of Appeal in May 2008, Justice Peter Leask was appointed as the trial judge. Before the proceedings began, the Crown stayed the charges against Azeroual. Three others—Brown, Barroby and Ayach—pleaded guilty for their roles in distributing the crystal meth in deals brokered by police agent Michael Plante.

Ayach was a drug dealer for the East End Hells Angels. He also collected debts for the chapter by seizing and selling drug debtors' property, with the proceeds going to the Hells Angels. His collection methods often entailed physical harm or threats of harm. Four months before pleading guilty to the E-Pandora charges, Ayach was sentenced to four years in prison for kidnapping and aggravated assault. The offenses were unrelated to the E-Pandora investigation, but the latter case would be brought up as part of a novel defense argument at Ayach's sentencing hearing.

The kidnapping stemmed from a dispute between one Ryan Danchuk and Ayach. They had known each other for years, but became embroiled in a disagreement over a $200 debt. Danchuk later admitted to police that he had said to a friend that he had a bullet for Sam Ayach and vowed to shoot him in the head. This got back to Ayach, who tracked Danchuk down, finding him asleep in a car parked in front of a friend's home in Port Coquitlam, a suburb of Vancouver, on June 22, 2005.

Ayach got on the phone and ordered three criminal associates to kidnap Danchuk, take him to a remote location and beat him. The trio dragged Danchuk from his car, kicked him in the head and threw him into their van, where they bound his wrists behind his back and covered his eyes with duct tape. They took him to a muddy construction site in a residential neighborhood of Port Coquitlam, where Danchuk was thrown from the van and immediately punched and kicked. During the beating, the duct tape slipped from his eyes and he was able to identify Ayach as the person who kicked him in the head while saying, "Are you going to shoot me now, Ryan?"

Danchuk managed to break away and ran toward the lights of nearby houses. He fell, was recaptured and stabbed 10 times before the group got into their vehicles and drove off. The knifings pierced his liver and punctured a lung. Danchuk survived the assault.

When he was arrested and charged with kidnapping, Ayach broke down crying while being interrogated by police. He also cooked up a phony alibi. After he was granted bail, Ayach was arrested the next month, along with Potts and Punko, for meth trafficking.

Back in custody on the E-Pandora charges, Ayach used another inmate's phone access card to call Danchuk—a violation of a no-contact order that was part of his initial bail conditions. He apologized to Danchuk for what happened, saying he never intended for Danchuk to be stabbed. Ayach suggested Danchuk should phone Ayach's lawyer to discuss the evidence he would give against Ayach at the preliminary hearing.

Danchuk, fearing further retaliation, failed to show up at the preliminary inquiry; he was subsequently arrested on a material witness warrant. He testified that he had no memory of being kidnapped and beaten, which the judge decided was a fabrication, since the victim had given a detailed account to police.

Ayach eventually pleaded guilty to the kidnapping and aggravated assault charges. Before Ayach's sentencing hearing, the defense retained Dr. Robert Ley, a clinical psychologist, to assess Ayach's psychological state at the time of the offenses. Ley's opinion was that Ayach was suffering from post-traumatic stress disorder, anxiety and clinical depression arising from his role in the Project E-Pandora investigation. Ley attributed most, if not all, of Ayach's symptoms to the harm Ayach allegedly received at the hands of Michael Plante, whom Ayach believed was a member of the East End Hells Angels. Ley concluded that, "Ayach was psychologically traumatized by the undercover operation and the threats, intimidation, assaults and robbery that he claimed Mr. Plante had inflicted upon him."

The sentencing judge, B.C. Supreme Court justice Daphne Smith, observed that the police tapes of Ayach's intercepted phone calls did not reflect that distress. "Mr. Ayach comes across in those calls as a violent gangster, who was completely adapted to the criminal drug subculture, and who had no hesitation in issuing threats of bodily harm or death to those individuals who were under his control," the judge concluded, sentencing Ayach to four years in prison for the kidnapping and beating.

• • •

Chad Barroby, another Hells Angels associate, eventually admitted he delivered 26 ounces of cocaine to police agent Michael Plante in Surrey in October 2004 on behalf of another Hells Angels member, who was paid $28,000 for the drugs. Federal prosecutor Martha Devlin asked the court to impose a three-year prison term on Barroby, but Justice Peter Leask imposed an 18-month conditional sentence of house arrest and a 10-year firearm prohibition.

Justice Leask had a history of controversial decisions involving drug traffickers, one of which involved Glen Hehn, a Hells Angels Nomads chapter member. He was acquitted by Leask in 2007 of allegedly possessing 52 kilograms of cocaine for trafficking. The drugs were estimated to be worth $1.5 million.

Hehn said he gave an acquaintance, Ewan Lilford, a key to Hehn's storage locker and the pass code to the entrance gate.

On July 21, 2003, Lilford arrived at Hehn's White Rock home and they traveled to the storage locker. Hehn retrieved a dog kennel and two children's lifejackets, putting them in the back of his pickup truck. Lilford got two boxes and put them in the truck. The two men then drove off. Police, who had Lilford under surveillance, pulled the truck over.

Police seized a cardboard box containing 22 one-kilogram packages of cocaine and a bright blue box containing nine one-kilogram bricks of cocaine. Police later searched the storage locker and found a nylon hockey bag containing 19 one-kilogram bricks of cocaine and a shoe box containing two one-kilogram packages of powdered cocaine. All of the drugs were stamped with the Coca-Cola trademark. Hehn denied any knowledge of the cocaine being stored in his locker. Leask found Hehn to be a "good witness" who gave clear and straightforward answers.

But what got Leask into hot water was a pointed response to Crown Prosecutor Ernie Froess. When Froess began making his final arguments in the case and suggested that Hehn's explanation was not credible, the judge swore four times. When Froess argued that the storage locker rented by Hehn contained a large amount of cocaine, Leask responded by saying: "But to be really clear, he'd have had to have been out of his fuckin' mind to store it in his own locker, all right? I mean, that's for sure, he wouldn't do that. Let's not spend any time on that theory."

Unfortunately, Leask uttered this and other profanities in front of a group of school children, who were sitting in the public gallery to learn about justice.* The judge's swearing created a public furor, with bloggers saying Leask should be fired. Leask quickly issued an apology for his swearing, which he admitted was "inexcusable." He said he deeply regretted his actions and did

---

* *Vancouver Sun* reporter Kim Bolan broke the story about Leask's swearing.

not want his conduct to damage the reputation of the rest of the judiciary.

While Hehn was acquitted, Lilford pleaded guilty to possession of cocaine for the purposes of trafficking, the charge that arose from the storage locker investigation. Lilford also entered another guilty plea for another U.S. drug case, netting him a 16-year prison sentence.

. . .

David Pearse and Kerry Ryan Renaud, the meth cooks in the E-Pandora case who were co-accused with Punko and Potts, also pleaded guilty.

Renaud had been sentenced previously to three years in prison as a meth cook. He was caught after a fire broke out on the eighth-floor apartment in a 20-story building in Surrey and a resident called 911. Renaud tried to flee from police, who found six kilograms of methamphetamine in the finishing stages—turning the meth into crystals—as well as the equipment and ingredients to produce more.

B.C. Supreme Court justice Frank Maczko, who imposed the sentence on Renaud in 2006, said he took into account Reanud's age at the time (he was then 26) and the fact it was a first offense.

"There can be no doubt that methamphetamine is a terrible scourge and that production of it ultimately causes severe and lasting harm to users of the drug, and that clandestine drug laboratories pose a grave danger of explosion, fire and release of toxic gases," Maczko said while sentencing Renaud.

The meth cook was on bail for that crime when he was busted in the E-Pandora investigation. At his sentencing hearing for the new crimes, the Crown contended Renaud was in charge of a crew capable of producing about 15 kilograms of the drug every 10 days, which could be sold for $13,000 a kilo.

At one point in June 2004, police executed a search warrant on an Abbotsford barn at 6521 Little Street that Renaud was using as an illegal lab, but he had moved nine buckets of crystal meth to another location before the raid, prosecutor Martha Devlin told the court.

"We don't know where the other cooks were done, other than the barn in Abbotsford," Devlin told Justice Peter Leask. "He had a central role in this criminal enterprise.... [Renaud] didn't seem too worried about the harm the drug would do to users." The prosecutor urged the court to impose an eight-year prison term to run consecutively with the three years Renaud was already serving.

At the time Renaud was arrested in 2005, the maximum sentence for producing methamphetamine was 10 years in prison, but a month later the federal government increased the maximum possible penalty to life in prison, the prosecutor told the judge. Devlin said the court needed to send a clear message that with the use of crystal meth on the rise in metro Vancouver, the authorities would respond by imposing lengthy sentences on those who produce it.

The judge read portions of a letter written by Renaud, who said he was "blinded by the easy money" and ignorant of the impact of his actions on society. "My greediness has done a lot of damage to a lot of innocent people. It definitely was not worth it," the letter said.

Leask said Renaud was one of a "relatively rare" number of inmates who see the light during incarceration. "I believe Mr. Renaud will probably not reoffend," he said.

Pearse, who also expressed remorse to the court, admitted he cooked meth and obtained the chemicals required for production, but was not involved in the distribution of the finished product. The federal Crown sought a jail term of eight years for Renaud, because he committed his offenses while on bail on the previous drug charges, and six years for Pearse, with the defense arguing that Renaud should get six years and Pearse three.

Leask sentenced Renaud to six years in jail but gave him credit for a total of 40 months for pretrial custody, reducing the sentence to 28 months. Pearse was sentenced to four years with credit for 28 months pretrial custody and an additional six months deducted for strict bail conditions, which was an unusual move. The meth cooks also received lifetime bans on possessing firearms.

(At the time, judges routinely gave "double credit" for "dead time" served in pretrial custody because there are no rehabilitation programs for prisoners in remand custody. The federal Conservative government changed the law in February 2010, eliminating the "two-for-one" credit, which had outraged many Canadians for years, although judges are still allowed to give credit of 1.5 days for every day served in pretrial custody in "extenuating circumstances.")

"Canadians lose faith in the criminal justice system when they feel that the punishment does not fit the crime. They have told us they want criminals—particularly violent offenders or those involved in gangs and organized crime—to serve a sentence that is proportionate to the severity of their crimes," federal Justice Minister Rob Nicholson said when the new *Truth in Sentencing Act* came into force.

• • •

In the months to come, there would arise more controversy about the sentences imposed by Justice Leask on the remaining Hells Angels facing trial.

By now, three years had passed since the E-Pandora charges had been laid and there were two remaining trials: Potts, Punko and Ghavami were the remaining co-accused in charges related to meth production and distribution, the last federal drug trial. And four full-patch Hells Angels members—Potts, Punko, Violette and Lising—were still facing extortion and weapons charges, which would be prosecuted by the provincial Crown.

Ghavami made an application before Justice Leask that the charges relating to the crystal meth should be stayed because his constitutional right to a speedy trial had been violated by the length of time that had passed before trial. The judge agreed, staying the charges against Ghavami, whom the Crown alleged was not the brains behind the crystal meth production but who actively participated in the plan to produce and distribute meth—the Crown's theory was that Ghavami handled almost $100,000 in cash and at least 14 kilograms of methamphetamine over an 11-month period.

The Supreme Court of Canada has made a number of precedent-setting rulings on what is considered reasonable delay in getting a charge to trial. The court found that a delay of 10 months can be reasonable, but in matters involving anything beyond that time frame, the issue of delay could be raised and could lead to charges being stayed. The nation's highest court has also stated that the delay must be caused by the Crown, whether due to a lack of resources or institutional delay caused by a backlog of cases.

In one of its landmark rulings, in a case known as Askov, the nation's top court said this about the problem of trial delay: "The failure of the justice system to deal fairly, quickly and efficiently with criminal trials inevitably leads to the community's frustration with the judicial system and eventually to a feeling of contempt for court procedures. When a trial takes place without unreasonable delay, with all witnesses available and memories fresh, it is far more certain that the guilty parties who committed the crimes will be convicted and punished and those that did not will be acquitted and vindicated. It is no exaggeration to say that a fair and balanced criminal justice system cannot exist without the support of the community. Continued community support for our system will not endure in the face of lengthy and unreasonable delays."

It has been a vexing issue for many years as the number of "mega-trials" increase. In the days before Canada introduced the Charter of Rights and Freedoms in 1982, a two-week trial was a long case. But now many criminal cases take two years or more, especially complex organized crime cases involving multiple co-accused, such as the E-Pandora case.

In November 2010, the federal government unveiled the *Fair and Efficient Trial Act*, which introduced a new approach to reduce the number of lengthy criminal trials that stretch on for years, causing some cases to be thrown out because of delay. Mega trials also eat up huge amounts of tax dollars. The new bill would allow for joint hearings when similar evidence is to be presented at separate but related cases, such as the multiple Hells Angels trials, to reduce duplication, court time and costs. But the new act came too late for the E-Pandora prosecutions.

After Ghavami's charges were stayed by Leask, the Crown launched an immediate appeal, which would take months to be heard.

The Potts and Punko drug trial was being delayed by pretrial motions, which was affecting the ability of the Crown to proceed on the weapons and extortion trial involving four Hells Angels. Because it was a jury trial, it was decided that the provincial prosecution would proceed first.

One of the concerns was that if the provincial Crown trial lasted the eight months that was set aside for it (or longer), some of the jurors might get sick and be unable to complete their jury duty. If more than two jurors drop out of a trial, for personal or health reasons, a mistrial can be declared, forcing the trial to restart with a new jury.

Before the 12 jurors were selected on May 18, 2008, for the trial of Hells Angels members Ronaldo Lising, Randy Potts, John Punko and Jean Violette, Violette applied to delay the start of the case by six months because of his deteriorating health—he is diabetic and wanted to get his blood sugar levels under control. He presented the evidence of doctors, who stated that because of bail conditions confining him to virtual house arrest, the accused had to be inactive. His weight had jumped from 200 to 225 pounds, worsening his condition, the court was told.

The judge, pointing out that Violette's bail conditions had been varied to allow him to work out at a gym and go for walks, denied the application. Potts and Punko remained in custody after being denied bail.

After hearing legal arguments, the judge also denied a challenge to the legality of the wiretap.

The trial judge, B.C. Supreme Court justice Selwyn Romilly, then heard a constitutional challenge of the criminal organization charges in relation to the four bikers. The defense argued the so-called gangsterism charges, created in 1997 and reviewed in 2001, which make it illegal for three or more people working together to commit a crime for a crime group, were too vague and overly broad.

"Defence counsel submit that notwithstanding the intelligence of Canadian juries, the mental gymnastics which will be expected of the jurors in a criminal organization prosecution are likewise absurd," the judge said during his ruling on the defense application.

"They will hear months of evidence to the effect that Hells Angels exist to commit crime, that they are as a group capable of the most heinous acts, and then they will be told to set aside that evidence while deciding whether the accused persons are guilty on the substantive or non-criminal organization charges on the indictment," the judge said.

"In addition, the charge against Lising, Pereira and Punko, which combines conspiracy to extort with criminal organization, will be so complicated that few jurors would be able to manage the mental gymnastics required to differentiate what evidence is admissible to what aspect of this multi-faceted offence. This is essentially asking the impossible and it is a process that is so fundamentally unfair the accuseds' section 11(d) and 7 [constitutional] rights will be violated by an inevitably unjust trial," the judge said, summing up the defense position.

Romilly, in dismissing the defense application, pointed out that issues raised by the four Hells Angels members had been previously raised and dismissed by the B.C. Court of Appeal in a case known as Terezakis.

Tony Terezakis was a mid-level drug dealer and a Hells Angels associate who was the first person to be charged in B.C. on criminal organization charges. It was not alleged that the Hells Angels were involved; Terezakis ran his own gang. In 2006, Terezakis pleaded guilty to serious drug offenses—trafficking heroin and crack cocaine—at the beginning of his jury trial, and then was found guilty by the jury of numerous counts of assault, including three with a weapon, against 10 different drug dealers.

The circumstances of the case were shocking and bizarre. Terezakis made videotapes of himself beating low-level drug dealers he thought had cheated him. With a large gold cross dangling from his neck, Terezakis would interrogate his victims, then punch, kick or hit them with a metal bar while shouting out, "Praise the Lord!"

His estranged wife found the 13 hours of videotapes and handed them over to police. Terezakis testified he planned to turn the tapes into a reality TV show called "Bible Thumpers," which was intended to demonstrate the pain of drug addiction and what he called the "freak show" of people living in Vancouver's downtown Eastside. He said the beatings were staged, but the jury rejected his version of events and convicted him.

Terezakis admitted he was fighting his own demons at the time—he was a cocaine addict. He explained in his testimony that he took over the drug trafficking business from his brother, who died in October 2001 from a drug overdose, and carried it on as a family business.

He hired young men to sell cocaine and heroin out of two seedy hotels on Main Street in Vancouver—the American Hotel and the Cobalt across the street—and paid them $100 for a 12-hour shift. The dealers would replenish their supply of drugs from a "stash room" in the American—they would turn over cash and the person in charge of the stash room would maintain a record of drugs going out and the cash coming in. When Terezakis believed someone was "short" on drugs or cash, he conducted an interrogation of the dealer.

During the beatings, he would exhort the victims, while bleeding and recoiling from blows, to read the Bible and pray for forgiveness. "The Lord has given me authority to hurt you if you lie," Terezakis would tell his victims.

Terezakis' trafficking operation packaged the drugs off-site, in rooms in the Linda Vista Motel in Surrey and the Sleepy Lodge Motel in Coquitlam, where police made substantial seizures in 2002. A Vancouver police department undercover surveillance team observed at least 10 transactions per hour in the American Hotel and as many as 20 in half an hour.

Terezakis, a former corrections officer, had a previous criminal record for trafficking 20 pounds of marijuana, obstructing a peace officer and possession of a prohibited weapon. For the assaults and trafficking offenses, he was sentenced to 11 and a half years in prison. The judge gave five and a half years of double credit for the 33 months he served while in pre-sentencing custody, reducing the total sentence to an additional six years in prison.

The trial judge, B.C. Supreme Court justice Heather Holmes, quashed the charge of Terezakis heading a criminal organization after a pretrial defense motion that posed a constitutional challenge to the criminal organization provisions of the Criminal Code. The judge agreed with the defense that the criminal organization definition was overly broad and vague.

Defense lawyer Matthew Nathanson had argued that the gangsterism law, as written, would mean if three infielders of a baseball team were growing marijuana and discussing it during games, then the entire team could be considered part of a criminal organization.

The Crown appealed that ruling, with the B.C. Court of Appeal restoring the criminal organization charge. The appeal court rejected the baseball team analogy, finding that the infielders would be considered a criminal organization, not the entire team. Besides, the court found, "The team's purpose and activity is baseball, not the facilitation or commission of a serious offence."

"Criminal organizations work in many different ways, using many different techniques and people to accomplish their ends," Appeal Court Justice Edward Chiasson said in the unanimous ruling involving Terezakis.

"The object of the legislation is to dissuade those who can do so from instructing others to commit crimes for the benefit of, at the direction of, or in association with a criminal organization. They may or may not be leaders of the criminal organization itself. The objective is to prevent them from using their ability to give instructions to support the objectives and activities of the criminal organization.

"In my view, the language of section 467.13 is clear and meets the objectives of Parliament. In addition, considering the purpose of the legislation, the reach of this provision does not appear to me to be overly broad."

But Terezakis was not convicted on the criminal organization count.

• • •

Terezakis was arrested with a number of co-accused in a two-year police investigation code-named Project Ecru, described as a crackdown on organized crime and motorcycle gangs. The charges arose out of a cocaine and murder investigation in 1995, beginning with a 305-kilogram seizure of cocaine worth some $9 million at the wholesale level and $30 million on the street.

The first seizure was made by Chilliwack RCMP after a car was stopped by police on September 24, 1995. Police found more than 135 kilograms of cocaine inside the vehicle, which had been rented in Alberta. Two Quebec men were charged with possession of a narcotic. Then, five days later, the RCMP drug squad found 170 kilograms of cocaine along with an AR-10 assault rifle in a Vancouver home in the 2900-block of East Fifth. After the two drug busts, seven murders took place involving people tied to the cocaine trade and the same alleged criminal organization.

In December 1995, Eugene Uyeyama, 35, and his wife Michele, 30, were killed at their Burnaby home, which was set on fire. Eugene Uyeyama belonged to a criminal organization that believed he had become an informant and had tipped off police, leading to the cocaine seizures.

Then, in September 1996, five people were killed at a rural Abbotsford farmhouse: Raymond Graves, 70; his wife Sonto Graves, 56; their son David Kernail Sangha, 37; and family friends Daryl Brian Klassen and his wife Teresa Klassen, both 30. The

Graves were thought to be killed because they owed a drug debt. The Klassens, also involved in the cocaine trade, had just dropped by to visit the Graves as two hitmen—Bobby Moyes and Mark Therrien—arrived to carry out the contract killings, so the couple had to be killed as well.

Robert (Bobby) Moyes was charged with the five murders at the Abbotsford farm and the murders of the Uyeyamas. Salvatore Ciancio of Vancouver was also charged with the Uyeyama murders but was acquitted at trial. Moyes pleaded guilty to all seven first-degree murders and testified against Ciancio, saying that Ciancio and another man, Peter Chee, had hired him to kill the Uyeyamas. In acquitting Ciancio of the Uyeyama murders, the trial judge concluded the evidence, including Moyes' testimony, was unreliable, vague, confusing and inconclusive.

Ciancio was also charged with conspiracy to traffic cocaine in relation to the 1995 seizures, but the charge was stayed after his second trial ended in a hung jury in 2010, the same result as his first trial. Charges against his co-accused, Aviv Ciulla, were also stayed. Ciancio went through three drug trials and a murder trial and was never convicted.

Despite the failed prosecutions involving Ciancio, the Mountie who headed Project Ecru, by then-chief superintendent Bob Paulson, remained optimistic that the next East End Hells Angels trials would result in significant convictions and the biker gang would finally be declared a criminal organization.

• • •

The trial of the four Hells Angels—Jean Joseph Violette, Ronaldo (Ronnie) Lising, Randall Potts and John Virgil Punko—finally started on September 11, 2008, in the high-security courtroom at the Vancouver Law Courts.

It opened with Mark Levitz, the senior organized crime prosecutor for the provincial Crown, telling the jury that the Crown would be calling evidence to show that Hells Angels is a global criminal organization that exists to facilitate its members' drug trafficking and other illegal activities. "The Hells Angels is the most powerful outlaw motorcycle gang in the world," the prosecutor said during his address to the jury, outlining the evidence to be called during the months ahead. The proof of the East End Hells Angels' reputation for violence were the illegal weapons, ammunition, hand grenades and dynamite seized by police during the E-Pandora investigation, Levitz said.

He went on to explain that the key witness would be Michael Plante, whom he said had agreed to become a police agent and infiltrate the East End chapter. Plante was used by each of the accused to commit crimes, the prosecutor added.

The Crown took the jurors through the 28-count indict-ment, which alleged the East End chapter of the Hells Angels chapter was a criminal organization and that the accused com-mitted crimes of extortion, uttering death threats and possessing illegal weapons "for the benefit of, at the direction of, or in asso-ciation with a criminal organization, to wit the East End chapter of the Hells Angels."

Levitz explained that Plante signed an agreement that paid him $500,000 at the conclusion of the police investigation, plus another $500,000 after completion of all the court cases. He said the jury would hear how the police agent earned "official friend" status with the East End chapter on January 21, 2004, which meant he had official duties at the clubhouse such as cleaning, grocery shopping and security at "church" meetings of full-patch members.

The prosecutor said the jury would hear conversations involv-ing the accused and Plante, who wore a police wire when talking about drug deals, weapons and proposed beatings. "During this time, Plante was walking a tightrope," Levitz told jurors, adding the agent "took significant risks to his well-being."

The jury heard a great deal of evidence about the drug dealing of the Hells Angels. But the media could not report anything related to the drug crimes involving Potts and Punko—the judge imposed a ban on publication of that portion of the evidence, since the two bikers were facing a separate trial on the drug charges.

At the start of the trial, the defense lawyers urged the jury to keep an open mind and not judge the accused simply because they were Hells Angels members. After all, it is not a crime to be a Hells Angel, one of the defense lawyers pointed out.

Violette decided to represent himself at trial. The four bikers had negotiated for more than a year with the attorney general for enhanced legal aid funding. The attorney general finally agreed, but the deal required the accused to sign indemnity agreements for the public monies that were to be spent on the defense at trial. Violette refused to sign the indemnity agreement, saying it would cause financial ruin to himself and his family. As a result, he represented himself, although he retained veteran criminal lawyer Richard Peck to make a severance application—Violette argued he should have a trial separate from the other three Hells Angels. The application was denied. Violette then retained senior criminal lawyer Michael Klein as a consultant during the trial.

Since Violette was representing himself, he also made his opening address to the jury at the start of the trial. He was facing charges for the extortion of Glen Louie—the alleged drug dealer beaten on Burnaby Mountain for using the Hells Angels name without permission—and illegally possessing two unlicensed guns: a loaded .25-caliber semi-automatic Beretta pistol and a Ruger .357 Magnum revolver with readily available ammunition.

Violette told the jury his dispute with Louie was personal. He was upset, he said, that Louie was dealing drugs and using the Hells Angels name. As for the guns found in his house, he said, they could have belonged to a number of people who lived in his home.

· · ·

The trial lasted for 10 months, the jurors hearing the testimony of 61 witnesses, listening to 329 intercepted communications and examining 415 exhibits. There was a parade of familiar witnesses from previous trials, including by then-retired RCMP biker-gang expert Jacques Lemieux, who testified about the structure of the Hells Angels and how its members operate in small "cells" to commit crimes in order to limit the knowledge of their illegal activities, thereby reducing the chances of police detection.

One officer testified about a document seized at the East End chapter clubhouse that detailed the chores undertaken by prospects, including fixing the dishwasher, repositioning the television satellite dish, cleaning out cupboards, power washing the deck, cleaning the coffee machine and calling in the cleaning lady once a month.

RCMP constable Dave Brown, who was responsible for keeping track of the evidence seized during the clubhouse raid, also read a note listing the names of members wanting tickets for a concert by Metallica, prompting Justice Selwyn Romilly to ask if "Metallic" was a band, which prompted some chuckling. "Fortunately, there's no one on the jury as old as I am," the judge quipped.

Before the jury began its deliberations in early July 2009, the judge told jurors they had the right to disagree and if they could not reach a unanimous verdict on each charge against each accused, they must acquit. He advised the jury that they could request playbacks of witness testimony or ask the judge for clarification on how the law should be applied to the charges.

During three days of deliberations, the jurors were sequestered—kept in a hotel each night separate from friends, family and any outside influences—while they debated the evidence. If the jury could not reach a unanimous verdict, a mistrial would be declared and a new jury would be selected.

Two days into deliberations, the jury sent two written questions to the judge with respect to the definition of a criminal organization: "Is the 'three or more persons' referring to the minimum number of persons required to constitute a group or is having the three East End chapter of the Hells Angels members involved in the criminal activity enough to call the East End chapter of the Hells Angels a criminal organization as a whole?" the jury asked.

"The answer to that question is yes," Romilly told the jury when court reconvened on July 10. "The group alleged here is the EEHA, not a subset of its members. If you find that the Crown has proved beyond a reasonable doubt that the EEHA is a group of three or more persons then the 'group' portion of the definition has been proved," the judge explained.

The second question was more complex: "Is having the three EEHA members involved in criminal activity enough to call the EEHA a criminal organization?"

"The answer to that question is maybe," Romilly told the jury. "It depends on the findings of fact made by you. The criminal activity of any EEHA member can be considered by you, together with all the evidence led at this trial, in determining whether or not the EEHA is a criminal organization. I remind you that in making these findings you must be satisfied beyond a reasonable doubt, based on all the evidence led at this trial, as to the various elements of a criminal organization which are: that the EEHA is a group of three or more persons in or outside Canada who are connected to each other in that group, however organized, and the group, the EEHA as a whole, has committing or facilitating serious offences as one of the main purposes or main activities of the group's existence."

The judge continued: "You need not be satisfied that the only purpose or activity of the group is criminal, but rather that criminality is one of the main purposes or activities, and the group, the EEHA, itself or its members would likely receive, directly or indirectly, a material benefit from its criminal purpose or activity. The benefit has to be material in the sense that it must be important and can include, but is not limited to, a financial benefit."

The jury then resumed its deliberations.

• • •

Just before the jury returned its verdict on July 13, 2005, the Mountie who had headed the investigation said that a conviction on the criminal organization charges would be a major blow to the Hells Angels in B.C. "It would be significant and it would be devastating for the B.C. Hells Angels," said Bob Paulson, then-RCMP assistant commissioner in charge of national security criminal investigations in Ottawa. "They are indeed a criminal organization and they need to be caught and punished for the bad things they do."

But, and quite surprisingly to many, the jury did not convict on the criminal organization charges, greatly disappointing police, who felt the evidence at this trial was the strongest they had gathered to date. The jury convicted on only seven of 26 counts—mainly weapons and extortion offenses—but acquitted the bikers of all criminal organization offenses.

The four Hells Angels were delighted. They laughed and shook hands with their lawyers and each other immediately after the verdict.

"It's unfortunate the jury wasn't able to conclude what judges in other parts of Canada found—that the Hells Angels is a criminal organization," prosecutor Mark Levitz told reporters outside court after the verdict.

"We're grateful to live in a democracy and have a jury system," Potts' lawyer, Bonnie Craig, told reporters.

It was the second failed test case of the anti-gang law against the Hells Angels in B.C. But there was still one more to go—the drug trial of Punko and Potts. With Leask as the trial judge, however, the police and the Crown were not optimistic about getting the ruling they desired. Justice Romilly put over sentencing of three of the Hells Angels until July 22, 2009. Violette's sentencing was adjourned until November 2009.

After hearing the submissions of lawyers for the Crown and defense, the judge imposed the following sentences on the four bikers.

Ronaldo Lising, 41, was sentenced to two and a half years for possession of two loaded guns seized at his home—a Rossi .357 Magnum revolver and a Walther .380-caliber semiautomatic pistol. The gun crimes were committed while Lising was out on bail for cocaine trafficking, the judge noted; finding that was an aggravating factor.

The judge took into account that Lising had a grade 12 education and most of his gainful employment has been spent working with his father operating a vending machine and laundry business. At the time of sentencing, the biker was married with children—he asked the judge to ban the publication of the names of his children, which was granted.

Lising's criminal record included an assault for which he received probation; a series of charges from 2001, including cocaine trafficking, for which he was sentenced to four years and six months; charges of assault and possession of methamphetamine in 2007 (his sentence was another four years and a $600 fine); and a contempt of court charge in 2008 for failing to testify at Giles' trial (sentence: nine months). Before he was sentenced, he was in the midst of serving a combined sentence of nine years and three months.

"The evidence led at trial establishes that Lising is a proud Hells Angel. He sports a Hells Angels tattoo on his arm and is frequently observed wearing Death's Head earrings. His home is full of Hells Angels paraphernalia and there are Death's Head stickers on the surrounding seven-foot-high fence. Lising is also wary of police surveillance and takes steps to insulate his activities from them," Romilly said in his sentencing judgment.

"The evidence also establishes that Lising views the Hells Angels as a club that should be ready to do violence and membership in the club as an opportunity to make money," the judge added.

Lising, a member of the elite Nomads chapter of the Hells Angels, had been in custody since his arrest in 2005, so the judge deemed Lising should receive no credit for pretrial custody because he was serving his other nine-year prison sentence.

Randy Potts was given a seven-year sentence for controlling the arsenal of weapons that Plante held for him. It included four grenades, four silencers and six automatic weapons, including a loaded Colt .45-caliber semiautomatic pistol, an Intratec 9-mm machine pistol, a sawed-off Ruger .22-caliber semiautomatic rifle, a Franchi .22-caliber semiautomatic rifle, a Voere bolt-action rifle and a .44-caliber Ruger revolver.

The jury may have acquitted the bikers on the criminal organization charges, but Romilly found Potts, then 49, was holding the weapons for the East End chapter of the Hells

Angels. "The grenades Potts had in his possession have only sinister purposes: killing, maiming or the destruction of property," Romilly said, adding he wanted "to send a message that the possession of these types of weapons, particularly the grenades, will not be tolerated in this society."

The judge continued: "The firearms found in his possession constituted a small arsenal that could be put to use on very short notice. The fact that four of them had silencers suggests that these guns were not viewed as defensive weapons and increases the seriousness of this group of offences."

The only purpose for the weapons, Romilly, said, "is an evil one.... The fact that they were capable of being used on short notice is an aggravating factor. If these are both aggravating factors, it follows that the fact that they were kept so that not just Potts, but a group of men could wreak havoc with them on short notice, is also an aggravating factor."

John Virgil Punko, 43, was sentenced to 15 months in jail for illegal possession of a loaded semiautomatic pistol and a consecutive sentence of four years for counseling the police agent, Plante, to damage a Surrey home where Punko was trying to collect a large amount of money from Parminder Gill.

The court heard a recording of Punko telling the police agent to, "Go by and light it up," a reference to a drive-by shooting that was intended to send a message.

"The circumstances of this offence are chilling," Romilly said, noting that Punko had previously been convicted of issuing a death threat against a Crown prosecutor at another Hells Angels trial. Because Potts and Punko had served four years in pre-trial custody; however, their sentences effectively amounted to time served.

Jean Joseph Violette was sentenced to six years in prison—four years for his leading role in the extortion and beating of Glen Louie, and another two years consecutive for the illegal possession of the two guns seized from his home. The judge noted that evidence seized by police indicated that Violette, although he had been a full-patch Hells Angels member for only a year at the time of his arrest, was "a committed member of the HAMC." He added: "From the evidence that was adduced at trial there is an irresistible inference that Violette carried out some executive functions with the EEHA. In the EEHA office he kept a metal briefcase with quite a few of the club's most important files. Additionally, he reported to [Rick] Ciarniello on club activities such as votes on various issues and the status of Stanton's trial. In February 2005, Violette was the representative of the EEHA at a western Canada meeting which took place in White Rock and Vancouver. And finally, he was instrumental in having Louie disciplined by the EEHA..."

The judge also itemized the abundance of Hells Angels paraphernalia seized from Violette's residence—a Hells Angels blanket, an East End Hells Angels jacket, a Hells Angels red and white hockey jersey, an envelope addressed to East End Hells Angels from the Toronto Hells Angels, a photograph of Toronto Hells Angels members, a Hells Angels calendar for 2005, an East End Hells Angels gold ring, a black DKNY bag containing Hells Angels jewelry, 54 Hells Angels T-shirts, six Hells Angels sweatshirts and 17 Hells Angels button-up shirts.

"These items, taken as a whole, substantiate the evidence proving his dedication to the HAMC," Romilly concluded.

The court was told that Violette, 58, had worked in the diamond drilling business since 1982 and he had joined the East End Hells Angels because of his passion for motorcycles. He had been married for 28 years and, the judge noted, "an intercepted conversation that he had with his teenage daughter while in custody on these charges is quite moving."

The judge said he considered letters of support, submitted by Violette's friends and family, which stated Violette was a man of great integrity and that the allegations of criminal behavior were out of character for him. Still, Romilly found that Violette had used callous violence against Louie on behalf of the East End Hells Angels, which was sanctioned by the chapter president. He called it a "heinous crime" carried out by Violette with a "businesslike, impersonal attitude."

"Members of a group can cause far greater injury to society than can individuals acting alone," the judge added. "Society must protect itself from such groups' actions by demonstrating that the rule of law will prevail."

Outside court, prosecutor Mark Levitz said the sentences sent "a strong message of deterrence and denunciation, recognizing the seriousness of weapons offences."

Punko and Potts still faced trial for methamphetamine production and distribution before Justice Leask. Before their trial began, the judge granted bail to Potts but denied bail for Punko.

• • •

In November 2009, Leask heard a defense application to stay the criminal organization charges, arguing the jury at the previous trial ending in July had already determined the criminal organization issue, so Potts and Punko should not be punished twice. The defense argued that the Crown was attempting to re-litigate an issue that had already been decided in favor of the accused, so the charges must be "estopped"—a legal term meaning stopping the charges from proceeding to trial.

Federal prosecutor Martha Devlin argued that the criminal organization charges should not be stayed because the judge could not speculate on why the jury came to the verdict it did. In fact, she pointed out, the trial judge at the previous trial, Justice Romilly, had determined at sentencing that Potts held a cache of weapons for East End Hells Angels and the beating of Glen Louie was carried out on behalf of the motorcycle gang.

Leask reserved his decision until November 27, when he announced: "My decision is the Crown is estopped from leading evidence that the East End chapter of the Hells Angels is a criminal organization." He said Crown should not get "a second crack" at litigating this issue.

It was another devastating blow to the Crown and police. The oral ruling, seemingly the Crown's last bid to have the East End Hells Angels declared a criminal organization, was over in 10 seconds. The judge said he would provide written reasons at a later date. "Well, what are we going to do now?" the judge asked the prosecutor, who appeared surprised by the judge's smarmy tone.

Leask suggested to Devlin that she might want to talk to counsel for Potts and Punko about guilty pleas, now that the criminal organization charges were off the table.

Days later, on December 7, 2009, Punko pleaded guilty to conspiracy to produce and traffic methamphetamine; trafficking five kilos of cocaine; and possession of proceeds of crime totaling $387,140—$244,640 was from methamphetamine distribution and $142,500 was from the sale of five kilograms of cocaine to the police agent Plante.

Potts pleaded guilty to conspiracy to produce and traffic in methamphetamine; two counts of trafficking cocaine; and possessing proceeds of crime totaling $264,300—$231,500 from methamphetamine distribution and $32,800 from the sale of cocaine to Plante. The sentencing hearing was put over a month—to January 18, 2010, for Potts and January 25 for Punko.

Punko's lawyer, Richard Cairns, argued at the sentencing hearing that his client's sentence should be reduced because Punko was used by Plante to get to other more senior Hells Angels members in the East End chapter. Similarly, Potts' lawyer, Bonnie Craig, argued that Potts was seduced by the big money offered by Plante in getting involved in drug trafficking. She also pointed out that Plante fed Potts' addiction to Percocet painkiller pills. Punko's lawyer also argued the police conduct, allowing Plante to feed Punko's addiction to Percocet as well, should be a mitigating factor in sentencing.

Prosecutor Martha Devlin urged Leask to impose a 16-year sentence on Punko because of the seriousness of the offenses and his previous lengthy criminal record, which included drug trafficking and threatening to kill a prosecutor who handled an earlier Hells Angels case. She urged the judge to sentence Potts to 12 years in prison for his extensive meth and cocaine trafficking, plus his holding the cache of guns, silencers, dynamite and grenades for the East End Hells Angels.

Devlin also urged the judge to find that Potts' previous criminal record, including his refusal to testify at Giles' trial, resulting in a six-month jail sentence, was an aggravating factor. Potts' criminal convictions included two counts of possession of stolen property in 1981 in Kingston, Ontario (he received a suspended sentence, a $200 fine, plus two years of probation); assault and using a stolen credit card in 1991 in Oshawa, Ontario ($500 fine and two years probation); careless storage of a firearm in 2000 in Surrey ($300 fine and six months probation); and possession of property over $5,000 obtained by crime in Langley ($500 fine and one year probation).

•   •   •

On March 12, Leask announced his sentences: 14 months in jail for Punko, one year in jail for Potts. The judge said he reduced the two men's sentences after finding they were used as "pawns of police" to catch higher-ranking Hells Angels.

The sentences caused immediate public outrage.

Law-and-order bloggers foamed at the mouth, calling for Leask to be fired, especially with his history of acquitting Hells Angels Glen Hehn and other high-level drug trafficking gangsters, as well as the incident of his swearing at the prosecutor in front of school children attending his court.

But Leask provided detailed and rational written reasons explaining how he calculated his final sentences. He took into account a number of mitigating factors that resulted in the sentence reduction. "It is my view of the facts that Mr. Punko was a pawn in this investigation," Leask said in his lengthy ruling. "It was always the intention of the E-Pandora investigation to go after targets higher up in the EEHA. In addition, Mr. Plante was being paid for the number of targets he could ensnare. To do so, Mr. Plante started by working with Mr. Punko and Mr. Potts, who were considered 'low-level mopes,' and gained their trust in the hopes that it would serve as a gateway to other members," the judge found.

"In doing so, Mr. Plante supplied both Mr. Punko and Mr. Potts with drugs, free of charge, evidently to gain their favor. While this may be a legitimate investigative technique used by the police to be able to get at targets higher up in the Hells Angels organization, there is no doubt that this conduct had a negative impact on Mr. Punko, who was attempting to rid himself of this [Percocet] habit and should go to diminishing his moral culpability.

"While the evidence with respect to Mr. Punko's drug abuse was insufficient to allow this court to draw an inference that it affected his intent to commit crime, the conduct of the police, in supplying drugs to Mr. Punko, is a mitigating factor in this case."

Leask said he would have given Punko a six-year sentence for the methamphetamine conspiracy, five years concurrent for cocaine trafficking and three years concurrent for possessing the proceeds of crime.

The judge gave Punko a one-year credit for his early guilty plea, saving the court a three-month trial, reducing the sentence to five years in prison. Leask said Punko was also entitled to 34 months of double credit for time served in remand awaiting trial, reducing his final sentence to 14 months in jail.

Similarly, Leask said if Potts had been convicted after a trial, the judge would have imposed a prison sentence of four and a half years, based primarily on comparing Potts to the methamphetamine co-conspirators charged in E-Pandora. Leask found Potts less culpable than the meth cooks, Ryan Renaud and David Pearse.

The judge said he would have imposed a five-year sentence on Potts, "but I was sufficiently impressed with his rehabilitation to reduce that to four and one half years."

The judge also found that Potts' medical condition—his lawyer told the court that Potts suffers from chronic back pain and a recurring abscess on his buttocks that causes him considerable discomfort—made prison time, both in remand and as a convicted criminal, "substantially more arduous for him than for a healthy prisoner. On that basis, I . . . reduce his global sentence from four and one half years in prison to four years in prison."

Leask also deducted one year's credit for Potts' "express willingness to plead to all charges except the criminal organization count on his first appearance before me and his actual pleas as soon as I ruled that the criminal organization count was precluded," which reduced the sentence to three years.

While Leask found the police conduct while investigating Potts was legal and justifiable based on their plan to collect evidence against other targets, it was not justifiable if their only target had been Potts.

"In this case there is the added factor that the Surrey RCMP would have arrested him in April 2004 as a result of their methamphetamine investigation and his criminal involvement would have concluded much earlier without either the cocaine trafficking or possession of proceeds of crime charge. I believe that Mr. Potts should receive the same reduction in sentence that Mr. Punko did for this mitigating factor. The effect will be to reduce his sentence to two years of imprisonment," Leask said.

The judge also gave Potts one year of credit for time served on remand awaiting trial, reducing the final sentence to one year.

Outside court, inspector Gary Shinkaruk said there were obvious discrepancies between the sentences and the lengthy prison terms sought by the Crown. "We certainly respect the position of the court," he said. "Sentencing is extremely complex. I would never question what a judge brings down."

Asked about Potts and Punko being called "pawns of police," Shinkaruk said: "Investigating criminal organizations is extremely complicated.... We certainly worked within the means of the law."

Prosecutor Martha Devlin walked out of court without comment to reporters about the sentencing of Potts and Punko. Later that day, she filed notice in the B.C. Court of Appeal that the federal Crown wanted to appeal, seeking to increase the short sentences handed down by Leask.

As well, before imposing his sentence on Potts and Punko, the judge had congratulated Devlin on her success in the B.C. Court of Appeal earlier that day—the federal Crown had overturned Leask's earlier ruling to stay the meth charges against Nima

Ghavami because of a 44-month trial delay. The B.C. Court of Appeal had ordered a new trial for Ghavami, who had planned to go to law school.

"On balance, we are not persuaded Mr. Ghavami's right to a trial within a reasonable time was infringed," the appeal court ruled. "Forty-four months is a very long time. Mr. Ghavami has spent the majority of that time on strict bail conditions, although the limitations on his liberty were relaxed as time went on. When balanced against the public's interest in the trial of the allegations, the balance favors a trial. This was a complicated prosecution arising from a difficult investigation, alleging very serious misconduct. As it unfolded, it required the time it took."

On August 8, 2010, the B.C. Court of Appeal granted the Crown's appeal of Punko's sentence, finding Leask made three errors in principle in his decision, and handed down an unfit sentence, based on the harm such serious drug trafficking offenses cause to society. The Appeal Court, in a 2–1 ruling, more than quadrupled the sentence Leask gave Punko.

"It is my opinion that a combined effective sentence of eight years' imprisonment would appropriately reflect Mr. Punko's culpability in respect of the two drug offences," Appeal Court justice David Tysoe concluded in written reasons. "Mr. Punko is entitled to a credit of 34 months in respect of his pre-sentence custody, which results in an actual sentence of five years and two months."

In dissenting, Appeal Court justice Ken Smith concluded that he would have almost doubled Punko's sentence to 26 months because of the meth offense. "The costs to society of drug abuse and trafficking in illicit drugs are at least significant if not staggering. They include direct costs such as health care and law enforcement, and indirect costs of lost productivity," Smith pointed out.

Similarly in a separate decision, another three-judge appeal panel increased Potts' sentence for meth trafficking to five years, deducting one year of pretrial credit. Appeal Court justice Anne Rowles found Leask made many errors, but the most serious was not imposing a sentence proportionate to the gravity of the offense and the degree of responsibility of the offender.

In September 2010, three judges of the B.C. Court of Appeal dismissed the appeal of his conviction by Ronaldo Lising for possession of one kilogram of methamphetamine for the purposes of trafficking—Lising had ordered the kilo from police agent Michael Plante in 2004. Its ruling upheld the lower court decision by Justice Victor Curtis, who found the RCMP and the police agent acted within the exemptions contained in the Criminal Code that allow trickery and deception.

The final appeal concerning Leask's ruling that stopped the Crown from proceeding on the criminal organization charges against Potts and Punko was heard on November 30, but the Appeal Court reserved judgment until after Christmas. On February 10, 2011, a three-judge Appeal Court panel granted the Crown's appeal, finding that Leask's ruling on estoppel was "an error of law." The court ordered a new trial for Potts and Punko on the criminal organization charges.

CHAPTER 11

"He had the balls to strap on a wire . . ."

With one trial still pending, Michael Plante must wait for his remaining $500,000 in reward money from police, which is supposed to be paid at the conclusion of all the Hells Angels trials.

According to his handlers, he is a much happier man today than during his days as an over-stressed police agent inside the East End Hells Angels, knowing he was a step away from death if he made a mistake that would arouse the suspicion of the bikers.

"He is the master of his own domain now," said a senior Mountie who still has contact with Plante.

The Hells Angels East End chapter is still functioning, its clubhouse still operating. The E-Pandora investigation may have made the club smarter and stronger, now that they know the details of how police used a civilian to infiltrate the club. With each investigation and prosecution, they learn a bit more about undercover police tactics, surveillance and wiretap.

"The Hells Angels continue to learn from every court proceeding and adapt their methods of operation to keep ahead of law enforcement," inspector Shinkaruk told a House of Commons justice committee meeting in 2009. "Disclosure during court proceedings has given the Hells Angels a clear understanding of law-enforcement processes, techniques, policies, and regulations. They are keenly aware of our limitations," he told lawmakers.

Shinkaruk told the justice committee that there have been 28 major police investigations across Canada since 2001 targeting members of the Hells Angels, which he called a criminal organization. "In the 28 investigations, 241 members of the Hells Angels were charged with various offences, including criminal organization offences. The 241 charged Hells Angels members account for nearly half of the Hells Angels active in Canada. Of the 28 investigations, 22 resulted in criminal organization charges. As evidenced by these statistics, police investigations are making use of the legislation, demonstrating over and over that the Hells Angels and its members meet the criminal organization offence criteria," Shinkaruk said.

He added: "The criminal organization court proceedings have ranged in duration from seven months to 48 months, and the average length of a court proceeding is approximately 25 months. In addition to the lengthy duration of these trials, the financial burden is also substantial, generally costing many millions of dollars. These investigations and trials are taxing law enforcement financially as well as draining human resources, due to their duration and evidentiary requirements."

Shinkaruk went on to say that in an attempt to proactively gather evidence required for courts, police now actively recruit members of criminal groups to work as police agents and obtain the necessary evidence to support prosecution. "Police agents, while being an effective tool for law enforcement, also come with high costs. Agents require an increase in human resources during investigations, as well as incurring financial consequences. Recent investigations that have utilized agents have given awards ranging from $525,000 to $1 million. This does not include ongoing protection and witness relocation costs," the senior officer said.

"It is a costly venture for law enforcement and the taxpayer to continually present the same evidence to the courts to get the same desired outcome. The current reality is that each criminal organization ruling has no bearing on other cases. There comes a point at which the overall cost of continuously proving that the same groups are criminal organizations is increasingly hard to justify."

Shinkaruk suggested Parliament should make it illegal to be a member of a criminal organization.

E-Pandora didn't bring charges against all the Hells Angels targets, but it was successful, Shinkaruk said in November 2010, when asked about his final thoughts on the investigation and lengthy prosecutions and appeals. "It's not over yet," he added, saying he was still awaiting the outcome of the final appeal on the criminal organization charges against two East End Hells Angels. "I don't think, realistically, anyone thought we'd shut them down. Our primary goal was to disrupt the criminal organization, and that was very successful."

He pointed out that the wiretaps gave police new insight into how the Hells Angels operate in B.C. The crackdown also took some of the luster off being a member of the Hells Angels in B.C., he added. It used to be that becoming a member of the biker gang gave you a "gold card" to become a successful criminal, Shinkaruk explained.

But E-Pandora proved the Hells Angels in B.C. are not invincible, he said, which will cause new Hells Angels recruits to wonder whether one of their fellow bikers or criminal associates is an infiltrator working for police. "There's not as much respect and fear [for the East End Hells Angels] as there used to be, and that's bad for business," he observed. "You don't want to have some upstart wannabe challenge you. They're already living a high-stress lifestyle to begin with. The more friction and stress we can inject in an organization, the better it is [for police]."

Shinkaruk also pointed out that, as Hells Angels members age, they begin feeling the effects of years of living the motorcycle gang lifestyle, including back and kidney problems. "People are starting to look at the Hells Angels as old and has-beens," he said. Even for the bikers who retire, it remains stressful, because they still have to worry about who's going to come after them to even the score for perceived misdeeds from the past, he added. Some retired members, however, are living very well off the proceeds of their Hells Angels years, Shinkaruk admitted.

Still, he said, the investigation eroded the high status and arrogance of the B.C. Hells Angels to the point that many young aspiring wannabe gangsters are choosing to join the upstart Vancouver gangs—the Independent Soldiers, United Nations and Red Scorpions—rather than applying to join the Hells Angels and be put through years of subservience to full-patch members.

The senior Mountie who oversaw the investigation, Bob Paulson, was promoted in November 2010 to RCMP deputy commissioner at headquarters in Ottawa. Now he is responsible for federal and international policing.

Paulson said that while the E-Pandora prosecutions failed to have the East End Hells Angels declared a criminal organization, the $10-million investigation still had an impact on the Hells Angels in B.C. "It was a demonstration to the targeted group that they weren't untouchable," he explained. "It put the bikers in their place, knowing they're vulnerable. It got them looking over their shoulder."

E-Pandora also prompted a spate of other people to contact police and offer to work against organized crime groups, he said.

Like Shinkaruk, he didn't expect the E-Pandora investigation to shut down the Hells Angels chapter. "You're never going to succeed in taking the Hells Angels off the face of the Earth," Paulson said, "but we got some of them." He singled out the tenacity and hard work of federal prosecutor Martha Devlin in juggling so many Hells Angels trials, defense legal challenges and the subsequent appeals.

"I think she did an outstanding job," Paulson said, citing the positive results of the Punko appeal, which overturned justice Peter Leask's short sentence and substituted a sentence more than four times as long. "It went a long way in sorting that out," he said of the appeal.

He also credited Michael Plante for putting his life on the line and giving up any kind of private social life for almost two years. "He was trouble," Paulson admitted about Plante's hot temper, recalling Plante punched a hole in a wall one night and another time "kicked the shit out of his car we bought him."

"He was a different cat. But he had the balls to strap on a wire."

He recalled Plante was patted down at one point by Hells Angels members to see if he was wearing a listening device, but it was never detected.

The investigation made Paulson aware of the level of sophistication among high-ranking Hells Angels who were raking in lots of money and amassing substantial assets over the years. "For the guys that were earning, the sophistication was impressive."

Police continue to investigate a number of unsolved murders believed to be connected to the biker gang. The latest is Jules Ross Stanton, who was gunned down outside his palatial Vancouver home in the early morning of August 13, 2010. Shocked neighbors heard up to 11 shots and saw a car with tinted windows racing from the scene.

Stanton, 41, had been kicked out of the East End chapter three months before his execution-style slaying. Some speculated the Hells Angels may have eliminated him because he was drawing too much police attention, but Stanton had made plenty of enemies over the years.

On April 4, 2010, Stanton had been charged with possessing a dangerous weapon, possessing a weapon without a licence and possessing a concealed weapon. He was also charged with assault causing bodily harm related to a March 6 incident in Vancouver. Stanton had become so violent that Vancouver police took the unusual step of issuing notice to John Bryce, the president of the East End Hells Angels, that the chapter needed to rein in Stanton, who was terrorizing people in the community with his Hells Angels patch. "We advised the president at that time that it would be in his best interest to tell Mr. Stanton to stop doing that," Police inspector Brad Desmarais, the officer in charge of the gangs and drugs squad, told reporter Kim Bolan. "I don't ever recall a time when we approached a senior member of an organization and said tell your people to shape up."

That was two months before Stanton's latest spate of charges. "We did tell him that Mr. Stanton's behavior was unacceptable on a number of different levels and as far as I can tell, they chose not to do anything about it," Desmarais said.

• • •

Despite the E-Pandora crackdown, the drugs controlled by the Hells Angels continued to flow in B.C. Less than a year after the E-Pandora arrests, police arrested in Vancouver a pilot named Michael Russell, then 60, of Toronto, who police alleged had connections to the Hells Angels in B.C. and Quebec, and the Quebec Mafia.

Russell was among 20 people arrested in March 2006 after Quebec Provincial Police searched a number of businesses and homes in the Lower Laurentians and northeast of Montreal at the end of a two-year investigation code-named Project Piranha, which resulted in the seizure of 49 kilograms of cocaine, smaller quantities of hashish and marijuana, as well as 136,000 Viagra pills.

Russell allegedly used international connections to smuggle multi-kilogram shipments of cocaine to Vancouver, then transported the drugs by private plane to Quebec. Russell made regular flights across the country between Vancouver, Toronto, Montreal and the Okanagan city of Kelowna, in the interior of B.C., police said.

Among those arrested in Project Piranha was Salvatore Brunetti, 60, a full-patch member of the Hells Angels chapter based in Sherbrooke, the chapter that Kelowna Hells Angels member David Giles had ties to before moving to B.C.

Police also arrested Montreal criminal lawyer Louis Pasquin, now 50, who had represented Brunetti during one of the Hells Angels mega-trials in Quebec in 2002. He was also the well-known defense lawyer for the Cotroni Mafia clan in Montreal.

The police investigation found a close link between Pasquin, Brunetti and the network's ringleader, Louis-Alain Dauphin, 53, of Mirabel. At trial, the court heard how Russell had dated Pasquin's sister, who was living in Vancouver at the time.

Pasquin was convicted in 2009 of cocaine trafficking and committing a crime for the benefit of a criminal organization—the first lawyer in Canada convicted on a gangsterism charge. He was sentenced to four and a half years in prison. Pasquin, now disbarred as a lawyer, is appealing his conviction.

The court was told at sentencing that Pasquin acted as an intermediary between the supplier, Michael Russell, and the head of the organization, Louis-Alain Dauphin, who was sentenced to nine years. (Russell is still facing trial.) Police heard Pasquin speaking in code on the phone during the wiretap operation and observed the lawyer loaning his former house northeast of Montreal to Russell when he came to Quebec to deliver drugs. The case illustrates the connections the Hells Angels have across the country.

As the commanding RCMP officer in B.C., Deputy Commissioner Gary Bass said in April 2009, "The Hells Angels are one of the most significant crime groups in this province and this country. Not all of them are the most sophisticated criminals in the world but the organization brings with it connections and territory.

"The Hells Angels, historically, have been involved in many of the drug importations from source countries, getting the drugs into Canada, and then, once in Canada, the Hells Angels have connections in this province and across the country, really. They have connections right into all communities, maybe not directly through members but through their various connections.

"People look at certain members of the Hells Angels and kinda wonder what kind of a threat that person could be. It's the power of the organization and the scope of their connections that make them such a significant threat."

Bass said there are more sophisticated crime groups rising on police radar, including Asian gangs such as the Big Circle Boys, who are shipping the precursor chemicals from China to make crystal meth. But all crime groups have one thing in common—the ability to move large drug shipments with relative ease, he explained.

Police estimate only about 5 percent of drug shipments are intercepted by law enforcement. "Any time there is a significant seizure that you hear about—50, 100 or 200 keys [kilograms] of coke, 400 or 500 keys of pot, something like that—it's part of a big organization," Bass explained. "And when you get the top guys charged in that, you are doing significant damage to the organization," he added. "Ultimately, someone pays the price for that [seizure] and in many cases pays the ultimate price."

• • •

Despite the E-Pandora crackdown, the Hells Angels also continued their expansion into Kelowna—there are now 11 members of the Kelowna Hells Angels chapter.

There will always be new gangs that arise, resulting in turf wars, shoot-outs between rivals and retaliatory executions. But the Hells Angels remain the biggest and most powerful outlaw motorcycle gang in British Columbia. So far, no one has successfully challenged the dominant power of their patch.

INDEX